QUIET WATERS

Reflections on the Twenty-Third Psalm

Nov. 2019

Dear Hana,
May our Good Shepherd
lead you beside quiet waters.
              Blessings,
              Pastor Ramil

through the kindness of Marlene

RAMIL N. CARMEN

ISBN 978-1-64458-136-0 (paperback)
ISBN 978-1-64458-137-7 (hardcover)
ISBN 978-1-64458-138-4 (digital)

Christian Faith Publishing, Inc.
832 Park Avenue
Meadville, PA 16335
www.christianfaithpublishing.com

Printed in the United States of America

To my Good Shepherd who is the source of all the gifts and blessings that I need to complete this work. To Him alone be the glory!

To my loving and prayerful wife Eleanor, my obedient and lovely children – my daughter Elaine, and my son Ram.

Contents

Preface

*For from him and through him and for him are
all things. To him be the glory forever!*
—Romans 11:36

I can only attribute the completion of this book to our Almighty
God. I give Him the glory and honor alone, and I thank Him for
the wisdom that only comes from Him.

The Twenty-Third Psalm has been one of my favorite chapters
in the Old Testament. In the year 2000, years before I became a pastor, I remember my daughter was in kindergarten and their teacher
asked them to memorize this chapter. I brought my family with me
over one weekend on a business trip to Dagupan City, a small city in
the northern part of the island of Luzon in the Philippines, which is
famous for its beautiful sceneries and seafood products. Throughout
the entire duration of our trip, my wife and I helped our daughter
memorize the chapter as she needed to recite the passages that coming
Monday. All three of us ended up memorizing the whole chapter as
well. It was one of the most exciting bonding time we had as a family.

Since that time, the Twenty-Third Psalm was like a song that
seems to play in my head incessantly. It constantly reminded me who
God is in my life and it made me understand who am I in Him. So
I would say my journey in writing this book started way, way back
during that time. When I became a pastor years later, I had delivered
several sermons about the Twenty-Third Psalm, and the more I study
the chapter, the more it spoke to my heart. Indeed, the Word of
God *"is alive and active. Sharper than any double-edged sword, it pen-
etrates even to dividing soul and spirit, joints and marrow; it judges the*

thoughts and attitudes of the heart" (Heb. 4:12). I could say that this book is more than fifteen years in the making. I believe as early as that trip to Dagupan City and during our drive back to Manila, God had already planted a seed in my heart that one day. He will allow me and bless me to write and publish this book.

The purpose of writing this book is to share my reflections and thoughts about this wonderful psalm. With the help of the Holy Spirit, I hope this book can give enlightenment to mainly two groups of people:

First, to those who had totally surrendered their lives to Jesus Christ as their personal Lord and Savior, this book will help them know God more intimately as their Good Shepherd who provides for their needs and gives them peace in the midst of this troubled world and, ultimately, the assurance that He will be with them forever.

Second, this book will be useful for somebody who has been searching for his life's purpose and meaning and why it is very important to understand our deepest need for the Good Shepherd in our lives. This book will also help them understand those people who are professing Christians and their family called the church. I hope I am quoting it correctly, but French mathematician and theologian Blaise Pascal once wrote, "There is a God-shaped vacuum in the heart of each man which cannot be satisfied by any created thing but only by God the Creator, made known through Jesus Christ."

For generations, a lot of people had tried or attempted to fill up that vacuum and search for life's meaning and purpose from so many other things—career, wealth, family, power, authority, and even religion without recognizing that all they need is the Good Shepherd. Jesus Christ alone can certainly fill up that vacuum and satisfy that deepest longing in their hearts.

Writing this book was not easy as it went through many challenges. It was like preparing Sunday sermon that never ends with no idea who your audience would be. The only difference was that the recipients of this work will not be a congregation and will not necessarily hear the message from a preacher at the podium, but instead, they are readers who will most likely be in the privacy of their homes and in the solace of their rooms.

I believe that the reflections and thoughts that I had put into this book were revealed to me by our Lord through the ministry of the Holy Spirit in my life experiences, through reading His Word and from interaction with different people who had influenced my life one way or the other. While writing this book had tremendously benefitted me personally first and foremost, I hope that these reflections and thoughts will be very meaningful for the readers as well, combined with their own reflections once the Word of God starts to speak to their hearts. I pray that each and every reader of this book becomes a willing vessel that will allow the Holy Spirit of God to minister to them and to speak deeply within their own hearts and lives, as He did to me.

Quiet Waters will give us a more profound reflection of the Twenty-Third Psalm and will allow us to appreciate the peace, calmness, and even the abundance that can only come from knowing the Good Shepherd intimately—who He is and who He should be in the life of each one of us.

I hope that this book will open the heart of any reader to a new understanding of who God is in his or her life. I pray that most of them, as they read through the pages of this book—particularly the Scripture passages quoted herein—will find in their hearts the emptiness that only God can fill in and ultimately, for them to fully and truly surrender their lives to Jesus Christ. To God be the glory!

Acknowledgments

I thank my Good Shepherd for all these wonderful people He has blessed my life with:

The Carmen family in Nueva Ecija, Philippines—for my late parents Manuel and Mercedes and my late brother Jojo; for my two wonderful sisters Min and Nancy; my in-laws Rey, Katsumi and Remy; for my nephews Peejay, Micmic, Jun, and Kenji

My second parents in Sacramento, California—Jun and Lorie Celestino

Celestino, Junio and Samson families Quezon City, Philippines

This wonderful and vibrant church in Vancouver, British Columbia, Canada, that He has blessed me to be a part of—Word Christian Community Church (WCCC)

My co-pastors, church leaders and members of WCCC

Our church denomination Word International Ministries (WIN)

Our first Christian church family in the Philippines, Word for the World Christian Fellowship–Makati

My good friends who helped me publish this book.

Introduction

As I had mentioned in the preface of this book, when my daughter was in kindergarten, her teacher asked her whole class to memorize the Twenty-Third Psalm. I was not happy at first because I thought it was too much for them to learn, and they were very young. What I didn't realize was that little kids are like sponges; they have very good memory, and they absorb everything that anybody taught them. I remember the following weekend I had to go on a business trip to a city north of Manila, about six-hour drive going there. I decided to bring my wife and daughter with me, and during that six-hour trip, my wife and I decided to use that time to help our daughter memorize the Twenty-Third Psalm, and we ended up memorizing it as well. It was a pleasant experience for the three of us, and it was one of those moments that we will always cherish as a family.

Just like my daughter when she was asked by her kindergarten school teacher to memorize the Twenty-Third Psalm, I read a funny story a long time ago about a Sunday school teacher who decided to have her class remember the Twenty-Third Psalm so they can recite it individually before the church congregation the following Sunday. She thought the kids would not have a hard time because the Twenty-Third Psalm is one of the most famous passages in the Bible, so she gave the children only a week to memorize the chapter. One little boy was excited about it, but he cannot just learn the psalm. He tried practicing several times, but he could hardly remember the verses, it was just too difficult for him. Although he practiced and practiced, he could barely get past the first three verses.

The much-anticipated presentation day came for the children to recite the Twenty-Third Psalm before the church congregation. The little boy was so nervous because he knew he did not have enough preparation, and he was simply not ready. When his turn came, he proudly stepped up to the microphone and looked at the whole audience for a few seconds, and with a loud voice, he said, "The Lord is my Shepherd, and that's all I need to know!"

It's funny what this little boy did, but come to think about it, he got it right! Sometimes you don't have to study theology to get your theology right, like this boy. God is our Shepherd, and that is all we need to know! If we truly believe in what Jesus said in John 10:27, *"My sheep hear my voice, and I know them, and they follow me,"* then we would fully understand what this boy really meant when he said, "The Lord is my Shepherd and that's all I need to know."

Sometimes we complicate our relationship with God by creating an image of Him in our minds that makes Him not only as a complex, huge, and complicated being but also as a distant and unreachable God. We sometimes even hear or sing a song that says God is watching us from a distance. But actually, He is not. He is somebody who desires intimacy and personal relationship with each one of us. He is close to us more than we can think of.

A lot of people always try to look at logic and rationalize their faith, and this is why we get easily influenced by skeptics when they challenge the Christian worldview by saying our faith does not go hand in hand with reason or logic. They are wrong. A lot of people have a misconception of biblical faith, and I believe faith and reason go together. Faith and reason are not inconsistent with each other. I believe that even in the field of science, more and more scientists are embracing creation over evolution because creation has more rational explanations than evolution. We now have a lot of scholars and rational thinkers out there defending Christianity in universities and various intelligent discussions. We have the likes of Lee Strobel, Dr. Ravi Zacharias, William Lane Craig, and a lot of well-known apologists challenging atheists and skeptics with rational discussions and debates.

The Bible tells us over and over again that God desires an intimate relationship with His children, a very personal relationship perfectly demonstrated by a shepherd caring for His sheep. God being our Shepherd is one of my favorite metaphors about God, and this is the reason why I tried my best with the grace of God to write these reflections on the Twenty-Third Psalm. I love the shepherd analogy, and it is my desire for those who will read this book to internalize that analogy about God fully. Realizing that God is our Shepherd makes me smile whenever I read the Twenty-Third Psalm, and I hope that same experience resonates with every person who will read this book.

You know what is funny to me is not the metaphor that God is my Shepherd but the analogy that we are His sheep. I know, for sure that the psalmist compares us to a sheep not because we are cute, lovable, and cuddly or huggable but because it is necessary for us to depend entirely upon the Shepherd. Later in this book, I will devote a great deal of discussion about the shepherd and sheep analogy, and this will give us fresh insights about who we are in God's sight and who He should be in ours.

The book of Psalms is a collection of songs, poems, and prayers mostly written by King David, the second king of Israel. If you are not very familiar with the Holy Bible, you can find the book of Psalms as the nineteenth book in the Old Testament in between the other wisdom or poetic books like the book of Job and the book of Proverbs. The word *psalm* comes from the Greek word *psalmoi,* and its Hebrew word is *tehillim* meaning praises. A lot of the Christian songs whether old hymnals or contemporary praise songs that we hear today are taken mostly from this fantastic collection of psalms. It is nice to hear new melodies using familiar psalmist verses. As a music lover myself, I found the book of Psalms as emotionally engaging as it touches the reader's heart, and for most chapters, it provides us with connectivity and intimacy with the God who created and who owns the universe and everything in it. The book of Psalms mostly shows how the authors intimately communicate with God; and obviously, in any relationship, communication plays a crucial role. Only those people who are intimately connected will be able to communicate with one another closely. Whenever you read the book of Psalms, you will feel the connection and intimacy that the author has with his Creator. This book shows a mixture of emotions that probably no other book in the Bible can convey. In some chapters, you can feel joy and excitement; you can sense victory and praise; you can appreciate the gratitude and experience worship. In other chapters, you can relate to anguish and pain, and you can almost hear the cries and the lamentations. Sometimes the psalmist cries out to God why and questions Him for being so distant and quiet. It is indeed a very emotional book, no wonder a lot of Christian composers use this book for making songs, and no wonder King David is called the "man after God's own heart" having written the most psalms because from his writings he practically laid bare his heart for people to see. He placed his heart out in the open and worshiped his Shepherd.

All one hundred fifty psalms were written probably in the span of more than a thousand years by different people. Almost half of the psalms were attributed to King David. Seventy-three out of one hundred fifty psalms were said to be written by him. Two psalms were written by King David's son, Solomon, and one was believed to be written by Moses. The rest of the psalms were written by different people, mostly priests, and about fifty were not named or designated to any specific person. Some Bible scholars believe that King David wrote the Twenty-Third Psalm when he was a young shepherd tending his father's flock of sheep. The main reason for this assumption is because the Twenty-Third Psalm is a shepherd's psalm. However, most scholars believe that King David could have written the Twenty-Third Psalm when he was a much older man, probably during the time when he was trying to flee from being chased by his son Absalom. They said verse 5 talks about King David's enemies, which is highly improbable if he was a young shepherd. Absalom was trying to take over the throne from King David, and his men were hunting down King David to kill him like a wild animal, and this is not something you would read on a daily basis—a son trying to kill his own father. I won't be surprised hearing in the news that a son would take over his father's business or a son disobeying his father's wishes, but for a son to try killing his father is probably more in the extreme side. How much of a failure can you be as a father for your own son, your own flesh and blood, to want to kill you? I cannot imagine the state of mind King David had at that time—the imminent danger to his own life, the possibility of losing the kingdom of Israel whom the Lord has entrusted to him, the fear of losing his friends and family members, and the idea that his own flesh and blood is trying to kill him. He cannot possibly comprehend how his life would have ended this way although he knew that these unfortunate events in his life were consequences of his wrong choices. These circumstances may have prompted King David to write one of the most potent psalms ever written, the Twenty-Third Psalm. Probably the most depressing stage in his life has been used by God for him to write a very powerful psalm that will impact lots of people for many generations.

When a person is afraid, he tends to do desperate things. We often hear the saying, "Desperate times need desperate measures." In the case of King David, he may have been desperate with all the challenges he was facing during those times, but I believe those challenges brought him even closer to God. Maybe in his old age and in the midst of a challenging situation, he remembered how he was relating to God when he was a young shepherd. King David knew that when he was a young shepherd, he had simple victories in simple situations, and maybe he wished that his situation was as simple as then. It reminds me of an old popular song entitled "Try to Remember" by Harvey Schmidt:[1]

> Try to remember the kind of September
> When life was slow and oh, so mellow.
> Try to remember the kind of September
> When grass was green and grain so yellow.

Have you ever tried reminiscing about the good old days? I did and still do. Of course, not to the extent that I can't move on from the past anymore. It's just sometimes, remembering the good old days can make you smile especially if you can recall the funny things that you did and experienced when you were small. It's amazing to realize how simple our lives were when we were much younger and we definitely had less complicated situations and even fewer problems compared to what we experience now. I grew up in a small town in the Philippines with rice fields, trees, and farmers around me; and, yes, at that time, life was really slow. The grass was green, and the grain was yellow during harvest. Life was much simpler when we were younger. Most people in our town would wake up very early in the morning, usually at dawn. They'll wear their hats and jackets and drank coffee together in front of their houses. They also sweep the street and go to the farm together in groups. I remember I would go with my father to the farm when there was no school, especially during summertime. I remembered the farmers would chat about so many things on their way to the farm—about politics, sports, TV shows, and, of course, farming matters. I value the experience of chatting with older men; they never run out of topics. I loved staying overnight at our farm. It was so quiet, and you can only hear the sound of crickets and the night owl. When it rains, you can feel the cold, moist winds on your face, and you can listen to the rustling of the leaves and the gentle sound of the river waves. There was no electricity in the farm, and the most these farmers had was an oil lamp and a battery-operated AM/FM radio, which can only pick up a couple of channels. At some point in the evening, they would gather together and listen to radio shows playing live basketball games, or sometimes they listen to the news. Oftentimes the farmers had to stay overnight in the farm. They were not afraid because, during my childhood days, our environment was much safer. I loved to climb on trees and swim on the river. There was only one thing that I feared the most in our farm— snakes! Life was indeed much more straightforward and much slower then. No traffic jams, no pollution, no noise or smoke from vehicles, and we felt safe. When we were young, we didn't have to buy toys. Most of the time, we make our own toys. It was really fun and memorable!

Nowadays, everything is going on at a very fast pace. You can barely catch up with technology. Before you can fully figure out how to use your new smartphone, the phone company is already launching a new model. Life nowadays aside from being fast-paced, everything seems to be instant—instant noodles, instant message, ATMs, online banking, microwave oven, and when we need information, we can get almost everything from the Internet instantly. Everything seems to be at the tip of our fingers. The Internet is a very powerful tool for getting information. Children nowadays seldom play outside their houses anymore. They are usually in front of a screen, be it television screen or computer screen or their game console. Some parents of younger kids also find these gadgets as a cheaper alternative to babysitting. The kids in this generation define socialization differently; it is called network gaming. Sometimes we wish if we can just bring back time and stay young and go back to those old-fashioned ways of playing. Back then we played outside in the streets with real (not virtual) playmates, and we climbed trees and swam in the river. I remembered there was only one rule that my parents strictly imposed on me and my siblings: we just needed to be home by six o'clock, so we can have our family dinner together. No matter where we were, we would always make sure that we were home by dinnertime. No questions, no arguments, no overtime. We were also required to sleep during afternoons, especially during summertime. We called it "siesta." A lot of times my older siblings would sneak out so they can play. It was a very strict rule, and we can get spanked if we violate those rules. Being the youngest, I would usually rat them out. How I wish sometimes we can just bring back the time when we were younger, so we don't have to face all these complexities of life.

As we grow older, our lives seem to get more and more complicated. We assume more and more responsibilities. There are more decisions to be made and more difficult situations to face. As an adult, we have more challenges, more problems, and more circumstances to deal with. When we were young, all we worry about was the game that we will play in the afternoon. All we need to accomplish were our school projects and homeworks. During those times, we thought that the world was about playing and going to school was just something we need to do. Our world was too small, and nothing was really that complicated. Nothing was serious. We just had complete faith that our parents will take care of everything else. No wonder God wants us to have childlike faith—no pretensions, no markups; it's just all plain and simple "us." God wants us to look up to Him like a little child, giving Him full trust and confidence that He will take care of us in everything that we may ever need.

I would imagine King David was clearly reminiscing the times when he was a young shepherd looking after his father's sheep when he was writing the Twenty-Third Psalm. He was probably thinking how simple was his life then when compared to where he was at that moment. All he needed to worry about was his flock and maybe from time to time bring food supplies to his older brothers who were either serving in the king's army or probably tending their flock. He knew that his father, Jesse, and perhaps his seven older brothers would take care of the more complicated stuff. They were, after all, the older members of the family, and he was the youngest. He probably did not mind if he was not the "star" among his siblings, and he was just contented with being the youngest, doing the most insignificant work and the smallest contribution to the family.

Being the youngest of four siblings in my family, I had always known when I was young that my parents and my older siblings will take care of everything for me. And they did. They were always providing for my needs, and they were always there for me. On the other hand, being the youngest, I also get some hand-me-down stuff from my older brother. I never complained because I had very simple needs. My mother was a very hardworking dressmaker and I remember, we seldom buy clothes for ourselves. My mother would sew clothes for the four of us. My brother and I would end up wearing similar clothes, especially during special occasions. In some cases, my mother would accept sewing jobs from our neighbors during special occasions like Christmas, and she would make curtains for them. If she has excess fabric, she will make me and my brothers some polo shirts. It was hilarious because as we walk on a Sunday morning going to church, we would notice that our shirts were of the same color and design with some of our neighbors' curtains. It was really funny, and instead of being ashamed of it, we would just laugh about it. It was a tremendous blessing to grow up with siblings. When I was a young boy, my eldest sister will take care of giving me a bath even if I stank because I was playing the whole day. She would bathe me so well until I become squeaky clean and comb my hair several times. My older brother and my dad would always play basketball or chess with me. Those were some of my great memories of childhood. Even when I was growing up, my family had always been there for me. My eldest sister supported my college education when she was in her early twenties. She worked in the Middle East as a nurse. She never stopped supporting the family since then. Same with my other sister and my older brother. They were all willing to help in their own ways. My parents had made a lot of sacrifices as well just to provide for all of us. I believe that is what a family is all about. They help each other and share burdens with each other. I cannot imagine how my wife got through her childhood, losing her own mother at the age of seven. Sometimes, we tend to overlook our own families, our parents, our siblings, and even our own spouses and children because of too much familiarity. We become complacent and insensitive because they were just there. They are going nowhere. Until one day we realize that their time here on earth is over, then we end up having full of regret for not being able to express our love to them even more when they were still around. I hope and pray that this book may prompt you to realize how important it is to express your love to your families. If you have to stop reading at this point and talk or call your family to tell them how much you love them, please do so. It could have been so frustrating to King David that in his old age, one of his most significant problems was about a family member.

King David wrote this powerful psalm that has been quoted time and time again for many generations. The Twenty-Third Psalm has impacted so many lives, including mine, and it mainly talks about peace with God and abundance, but ironically it was composed by a man who was in the midst of grave threats and serious trouble.

Isn't this scenario true for most of us? Our creative juices flow when we are stressed or pressured. I knew some people who can write songs whenever problems come their way. When we are down and out and we are engulfed with challenges in life, don't we look up to God more often? Don't we pray more when we things seem not to work out well in our lives? When we are sick, physically or even emotionally, don't we call on to God for healing? A lot of people believe that the most sincere prayers are said in hospitals, and I believe it is human nature that when things are going well and smooth sailing, we tend to forget calling up to Him even just to thank Him. I have been approached by so many people asking for prayers, and in most cases, it is about sickness. The adage, "Health is wealth," is indeed true. I have also visited a lot of people over the years in hospitals, and it is true that you can hear the most serious and heartwarming prayers beside the hospital bed. When we are experiencing life like a bed of roses, in most cases, the last item on our agenda is a thanksgiving prayer or going to church to worship God. So from time to time, we need a wake-up call from God so we can get to understand the more important things in life and grow in our faith more when we are experiencing struggles and pain in our lives.

The Twenty-Third Psalm provides additional insights into difficult situations in life especially when it talks about God's rod and staff. C. S. Lewis in his book *The Problem of Pain* wrote, "God whispers to us in our pleasures, speaks in our conscience, but shouts in our pains: it is his megaphone to rouse a deaf world."[2] It simply means that the voice of God seems much softer, and we can barely hear Him when

The real challenge is not going through problems or difficult situations as all people go through that but how are we able to get out and be victorious in those difficulties.

life's pleasures are all that surrounds us. Imagine yourself in the midst of a noisy midnight party with all the merry-makings around you, with all the people talking at the same time, with all the drinking, loud music, and dancing. Then suddenly you receive a call on your cell phone from your father. I am pretty sure when you pick up the call and start talking to him, you can barely hear him, and probably your first instinct is just to end the call. He would probably try to remind you not to drink too much because you are driving, but you find it annoying as it ruins your mood in the party, so you hang up. Let us say for example you drank too much and ended up getting into an accident while going home. Probably the first person you will call is your father. This time, it's different. You probably would listen more and pay attention. This time you probably realize that had you listened to him when he called you earlier, you would not have gotten into that accident. If we are in pain and experiencing problems, God is already shouting at us. He uses those painful experiences to wake us up from a deep slumber or from being so complacent in our pleasures of life. I also learned over the years from experience that sometimes, God uses these problems and sad experiences in life for us to one day minister to other people and share the lessons that we have learned from those painful experiences. One day, we shall meet someone who is probably going through a similar ordeal in life. It will then be our time to share how did we go out victorious in that situation. The real challenge is not going through problems or stressful situations as all people go through that but how are we able to get out and be victorious in those difficulties. I always tell my children or even our church members to listen to godly counsel and understand what the Lord is saying through the scriptures. From these sources, we should get a pretty good idea on what to do in any given situation and learn our lessons from the truths spelled out in the Bible and from the experiences of others who have been there ahead of us. Otherwise, God will create situations that can teach us or wake us up. Hard as it may seem, but God is more interested in building up our character rather than to continuously supply us with the pleasures of this life. These seemingly adverse situations are like bitter pills that God wants us to swallow from time to time. These pills may not blend well with our taste buds, but each bitter pill we take is working slowly for our benefit and improves our overall spiritual health and well-being. God may provide situations in our lives that may not seem pleasant at first, but in the end, it will be for our benefit. We are familiar with the old saying, "No pain, no gain." I think this holds true when it comes to life's experiences as well. It is hard to learn something only in theoretical aspects. Even in school, the greatest lessons are learned whenever we have actual experiments or even do cooperative studies or summer jobs. Wisdom is found not in acquiring knowledge and learning things that tickle our brain, but it is the positive application of that knowledge in our lives. The Bible says in the book of Romans 8:28, "*And we know that in all things God works for the good of those who love him, who have been called according to his purpose."* The principle found in this verse gives us the assurance that if we love God and if we live our lives according to His purpose, all things that happen to us, whether good or bad, will eventually be for our good. These things will benefit us in the long run. Knowing this truth encourages us to persevere during trials and sufferings because we know things that seem bad at first are actually being used by the Lord, in His divine plan and wisdom, to accomplish something good for us.

It reminds me of a story in the Old Testament about Joseph, son of Jacob. His jealous brothers sold him as a slave to traders going to Egypt. In Egypt, he was imprisoned for a long time, but God had prepared something great for him. After so many years, God has blessed him tremendously as he became second to Pharaoh in Egypt, and when he had the chance to confront his brothers about what they did to him, he blessed them instead of getting revenge. He said in Genesis 50:20, *"You intended to harm me, but God intended it for good to accomplish what is now being done, the saving of many lives."* A lot of times, when we are still in the midst of difficulties, it's hard for us to understand why it's happening and its hard pick up the good things while in the midst of hardship. But it is more important to know that God, in His infinite wisdom and power, can use all these difficult situations for our own good. We may not see it all the time, but we have to trust God that He knows what He is doing.

Even before becoming a Christian, I have heard the Twenty-Third Psalm recited time and time again, mostly in funerals. People get too emotional sometimes when they hear this psalm. I remember reciting this psalm when my wife's nephew passed away when he was still a baby. The whole clan of my wife was there, and that was probably one of the first few instances that I spoke in public. Taking off from that experience when I became a minister, I have read this passage a couple of times during funeral services as well. I used to call it the psalm of the dead, especially that part in verse 4 when it mentions *"the valley of the shadow of death."* It is a bit scary and depressing if a young person will read that part. It seems like all it talks about is dying. But as I read and understood deeper, as I meditated more and more about the Twenty-Third Psalm, I gained a much better understanding. My whole perception has changed, and I think it was actually a psalm for the living rather than for the dead! It talks about eternal life and security in the Lord. It talks about the Lord bringing us toward the kind peace that He alone can provide and the abundant life that He alone can make possible in us plus the comfort in knowing that He makes us lie down in green pastures and lead us beside quiet waters! God is indeed able to do that. Nothing is impossible with Him. He can bring us to the kind of peace that we can never achieve through our own efforts no matter how much we try. He alone can give us the true meaning of our lives and the reason why we exist. After all, He is our Creator, and obviously, He knows how He wired us and how we can fully maximize that life that He has blessed us with.

My own life is also a testimony that during the darkest and most challenging stage of my family life and marriage, I came to know Jesus in a very personal and intimate way. I have heard from a lot of people how God loves me and how He desires to have a personal and intimate relationship with me, but sadly, I never listened. I believe that God called my attention and shouted to my ears through adversities. And I'm glad that He did not give up on me. I'm thankful that He did call me.

I believe there are a lot of people in the world today who are lost in the quagmire of trying to find out the meaning of their lives. They try and try, they search and search; but in the end, it's merely a vicious cycle that they got themselves entangled with. Some people seek life's meaning through worldly pleasures but I assure you they won't find anything there.

I hope and pray that this book will help you find what you are looking for in life and understand your deepest longings. I hope and pray that as you read this book, God will help you to open your heart and recognize what is missing in your life, and I have the confidence to tell you that these longings and emptiness can only be filled and satisfied by the Good Shepherd.

Reflection Questions

1. A lot of people search for something in this world. Some search for material prosperity, some search for prestige, some search for the "fountain of youth," and some search for perfect relationships. What do you search for in life?
2. If you are one of those who seek for relationships, what kind of relationship are you searching for?
3. Have you been through a really difficult situation? How did you get out of it?

A Man After God's Own Heart

One of the things I love about the Bible is the fact that it does not sugarcoat its stories, more so it does not paint its principal heroes or characters to make them superficially attractive or impressive. Their credentials were not inflated, and the writers did not "pick and select" the good side of their lives. The Bible presents its key characters for who they truly were, and this includes both their strengths and weaknesses, as well as their successes and even their failures. The biblical writers wanted to show us that these so-called biblical heroes, just like every one of us, at certain points in their lives have disappointed God one way or the other. I believe God allowed it this way for each one of us to be able to relate and identify ourselves with the biblical characters. God knows that we too have lots of flaws, and we too have weaknesses. He must know, as He created each one of us. The Bible heroes of our faith are not flawless or "holier than thou" individuals, but instead, they are just ordinary people used by an extraordinary God to fulfill His extraordinary plans. The Bible from the book of Genesis is full of misfits, but it is amazing to see how God has worked through them and carried out His plans.

In the Old Testament, we can read in Genesis 3 that Adam and Eve disobeyed God when they ate the fruit from the forbidden tree. It's funny because God gave them everything in the garden to enjoy except the fruit coming from the tree of the knowledge of good and evil, but the serpent tempted Eve, she ate the fruit and even gave some to Adam. The rest is history. The writer of Genesis did not decide to omit the flaw even from our very first parents in order for the creation story to make it to New York's top best-selling book or to score high points in popularity surveys. No, he told the story as it happened. You can also read in Genesis 20:2 that Abraham lied about his wife Sarah before Abimelech, the king of Gerar. He told the king, "She is my sister," referring to Sarah to save himself. I suppose a lot of people would ask, "Really? Abraham, the patriarch, lied?" What would the Jews think about this? But that was precisely what really happened and the Bible has a unique way of telling us of the flaws of each of these characters. Years later, when the angel of the Lord told Sarah that she would bore a son, she laughed sarcastically because she thought at her age, which was way past childbearing, how can she even entertain the idea that she will have a son. Just like anyone of us, she made mistakes. She did not patiently wait for God to open her womb and make her pregnant. She foolishly sent her handmaid Hagar to Abraham, which resulted in the birth of Ishmael, and this triggered a long-standing feud between the off-springs of Abraham's sons up to our time today. One generation later, Abraham's son Isaac committed the similar sin with his father when he lied about his wife Rebekah before the king of Gerar again. It certainly runs in the blood, don't you think? Another generation came about. Isaac's son Jacob lied to his father pretending to be his brother Esau so he can get his father's blessing. Jacob's sons sold their youngest brother Joseph to slavery in Egypt and lied to their father telling him the wild animals killed him by showing their father Joseph's bloodstained robe. This family is like a multigeneration of liars. But to me, the credibility of the Bible is not diminished even if these stories are there. The Bible shows us that these people are merely human and, of course, imperfect; but God had His reasons for using them, and because God is Almighty, He can to accomplish His will through them. We know that Moses tried to reject God's calling for him to free the Israelites. He said to God in Exodus 4:10, "*I have never been eloquent, neither in the past nor since you have spoken to your servant.*" What's interesting was the Lord's response. He said in the following two verses: "*Who gave human beings their mouths? Who makes them deaf or mute? Who gives them sight or makes them blind? Is it not I, the Lord? Now go and I will help you speak and will teach you what to say.*" But still, Moses didn't want to do it, and God's anger burned against Moses, so He asked for his brother Aaron. A lot of times, we waste an opportunity because of how small and how low we view ourselves. We focus on our weaknesses, but God is perfectly aware of that, just like what He told Moses. All we need to do is to trust Him that if He called us to do something, He will enable us and give us the power and ability to do it.

Later in Moses's life, as they were wandering in the desert, he disappointed God when he struck the rock twice in the waters of Meribah, and this action has cost Moses a lot as he lost the opportunity to step foot on the promised land along with the other Israelites who kept on grumbling. If God's intention when He inspires the Old Testament authors is just to promote some of the characters and make them celebrities or heroes, He would probably omit the problems that Moses encountered, specifically the incident in Meribah. He can just wipe them out from the pages of the Bible. But no, God has no intention to make its characters become like Hollywood celebrities and only Him, the creator of the universe and the enabler of all these so-called heroes must be glorified, and His name alone must be lifted up in any of the stories of victory that we can read from it. Whenever we read about their achievements, we will not be tempted to "worship" these heroes nor attribute their successes to their own abilities alone, but instead, we know that it was all coming from God. It's funny because if you read all those stories, you'll find out that God's specialty is to make use of the least-possible people and the least-likely people to fulfill His will and plans here on earth. Rahab was a prostitute in Jericho, and yet she was able to protect the two spies sent by Joshua to look over the land. Jonah was proud, stubborn, disobedient, and grumbling prophet. He ran away toward the opposite direction of Nineveh. Elijah wanted to die. His faith wavered, and he was depressed and felt sorry for himself. Samson was foolish and loved women more than submitting to God's will. But imagine how much God had used all these people to accomplish His purpose. God does not need people who are already so full of themselves. All God wants is a willing vessel, somebody who is more than ready to be used by God in whatever way He can. What we can be assured of is that the Bible presents each biblical character for who he or she truly is: no more, no less!

Even in the New Testament, we can read that even the closest disciples of Jesus Christ disappointed Him one way or another. No less than Jesus Christ trained them for three years. They ate with Him, they slept with Him, they weathered the storm with Him; and yet during the final hours of Jesus's life, the opportune time when they can prove their love for Christ, they started to do the unthinkable. One by one, they began to falter. Peter denied Jesus three times on the night of His crucifixion while Thomas doubted His resurrection and was asking for more proof. Of course, we know about Judas Iscariot and how he sold his master for thirty pieces of silver although this one was not able to recover at all. One of the most remarkable stories in the New Testament was the resurrection of Christ. From the stories narrated by the Gospel writers, the primary witnesses to the empty tomb were women. In those days, women were probably the most ill-perceived and "no credibility" witnesses that you can have. But instead of omitting this incident from the Bible, the Gospel writers made sure the women were clearly identified as the primary witnesses. Instead of ruining the credibility of the resurrection, it even strengthens its claim to reality. If resurrection is a hoax as claimed by the enemies of Christianity, why would God even chose women to be the first witnesses? Or if the disciples were just fabricating the resurrection story, why didn't they get credible male witnesses to make up their story? There is only one answer. The Bible does not sugarcoat its stories. It tells the story as they had exactly happened, and the characters are presented for who they truly were. God uses women to be the primary witnesses to the empty tomb, that's it. That's what really happened. You can either accept it or not.

The history of the world for generations is a history of deception and deceit. Since the beginning of time and down to modern-day settings, battles and wars were lost because of betrayal and deception. I remember when I was a young student studying Philippine history, I was shocked to learn that most of the battles or wars lost by the Filipinos were frequently due to deception by traitors. I have read stories about one Filipino defecting to the Spaniards and that would cause the defeat of the whole battalion of the rebel group. The Bible has clearly shown this sad reality in the various stories written and narrated by each writer used by God, one of which was the betrayal of Judas Iscariot against our Lord Jesus Christ. The Word of God also shows us that the enemy is always waiting for an opportunity to tempt those people who are primarily being used or will be used by God to fulfill His purpose. So don't be surprised if this happens to you as well. As you start to get yourselves more and more involved in serving the Lord, the enemy will now start working double time in order to cast doubts on you, confuse you, and even bring sufferings to discourage the children of God to be productive in their Christian walk. Every time a child of God rises to more significant challenges the enemy is putting a mark on him or her. The enemy's goal is to make the lives of God's children miserable to the point that they will start to doubt themselves if they indeed are Christians.

King David, our psalmist, and writer of the Twenty-Third Psalm is no exception. The Bible presents him for who He truly was—anointed by God through Prophet Samuel at a young age to be the next king of Israel. Sometimes even during our time today, we see or meet some accomplished people and well-known individuals. Our reaction is usually looking at the person as if he had always been that successful. But little did we know that what we see at present could be just a fruit of all the sacrifices that this person has done all his life. Sometimes, what we see now is a result of too many sacrifices done in that family for several generations.

King David was an outstanding shepherd when he was much younger and later was known as a courageous and loyal soldier. He became a great warrior and king, but he disappointed God when he committed grave sins such as adultery with Bathsheba and mur- der for causing the death of her husband Uriah who was one of his loyal and brave soldiers. King David thought that he can get away from being haunted by his sins of adultery and the death of Uriah. Sometime later, he was rebuked by the Prophet Nathan, and he even- tually repented of all his wrongdoings; but of course, he still had to suffer severe consequences. We thought if we repent or if we ask for forgiveness, we can already escape the results of our past sins. We need to face and accept the consequences of our sins because it is good for us. It teaches us great and priceless lessons in life as we experience those pain and sufferings because of something wrong we did in the past. Chances are, we will most likely do better next time. God can also use these experiences so He can use us and our experiences to minister or disciple other people who are in a similar situation.

The reason why King David is one of my favorite biblical characters is that he is presented in the Bible for who he truly is. I can relate to him personally because like him, I also had a lot of issues in my past, and sometimes even in my present life, that for sure disappoint God over and over again. Like King David, I also have lots of flaws and weaknesses. We always fall short of His standards. If you read King David's story, you will learn that God is indeed a God of second chances. With His arms open wide, He is always there and ready to receive us back and gives us a second chance. He has given King David the opportunity to recover from his situation and sincerely repent of his sins. God knows that His children will always have the propensity to commit mistakes and will cause Him disappointments, but He always offers back love and understanding, and He is always ready to give second chances and ways for us to bounce back. God is always ready to forgive our sins because Jesus had already paid the price for our redemption and forgiveness of our sins—past, present, and future!

> **God is always ready to forgive our sins because Jesus had already paid the price for our redemption and forgiveness of our sins—past, present, and future!**

King David was first mentioned in the Old Testament in the book of First Samuel sixteenth chapter when the Lord anointed him through the prophet Samuel. He was the youngest of the eight sons of Jesse. It is also interesting to know that King David was the great-grandson of Ruth, the Moabite. Ruth married Boaz, guardian-redeemer, and they had a son named Obed, who was the father of Jesse.

While the Bible described him as somebody with an appearance that is *"glowing with health and had a fine appearance and handsome features"* (1 Samuel 16:12); however, he still probably fell short or he thought he was not at par with the qualities of his other brothers in terms of overall physical appearance especially his height and probably even strength. I would imagine that his older brothers are more superior in terms of physique; no wonder they can well serve in King Saul's army. One of the most important lessons in the early life of King David was when the Lord reminded Samuel not to be influenced by what he will see in the outside, but instead, God told Samuel that *"People look at the outward appearance, but the Lord looks at the heart."* This was written in 1 Samuel 16:7. How many of us are easily influenced by what we see or hear in the outside? How many of us are easily influenced by our five senses? A lot of times we can discriminate individuals merely by their physical appearance or by their gender, race, social status, and even by their financial condition. I have experienced this being an immigrant to the nation where I live now. People sometimes look down on you even before they get to know you as a person. They judge you by your appearance. Do you wear fine clothes or speak good English or drive a nice car or did you get a good education? Sometimes we also get stereotyped because we belong to a particular minority race or nationality. It is sad that even before we open our mouths, some people already have preconceived notions about us. They are already prejudging us about what we can or cannot do. Sometimes not because of their own experience but based on what they read or what other people tell them.

Upon reading the story of King David, now I know why we sometimes judge one another based on what is seen from the outside. Humanity, because of our fallen state, has all the inclination to look only at the outside appearance and we are sometimes too quick to judge a person based merely on what we see or hear. No wonder we oftentimes quote the popular English idiom, "Do not judge the book by its cover." It also reminds me of the popular Disney movie *Beauty and the Beast* which is the favorite of my daughter where the enchantress reminded the proud prince "not to be deceived by appearances for beauty is found within." King David was anointed by God through the prophet Samuel to be the second king of Israel, but it took him more than fifteen years before he finally sat on the throne. That's a long wait. I wonder how many of us can have the patience to wait that long.

The Bible also tells us that King David was not only a shepherd as the servants of the kingdom described him as a brave man and a warrior. He was also a fine musician as he knew how to play the lyre, and of course, he wrote many psalms. The first king of Israel Saul regularly summoned King David and had him play the lyre whenever he feels being tormented by evil spirits. King David became Saul's total entertainer. King David's music provided nourishment to the soul of Saul! God has blessed King David to become a musically gifted person, no wonder he penned most of the psalms in the Old Testament. Some writers would depict King David as if he was a very young weakling, but actually, King David was a physically fit individual; and being a shepherd, he should be very strong. Otherwise, how was he able to protect his flock from wild animals? He also became one of King Saul's armor-bearers, so I cannot imagine how a weakling can carry the heavy metal armor of the king. The famous sculptor Michaelangelo of the Renaissance period created a masterpiece sculpture of King David when he was commissioned by the Opera Board in Florence, Italy, and this renowned sculpture depicted King David as a very handsome and physically strong individual. The statue stood more than five meters and was made of marble. The sculpture showed King David prior to engaging his battle with Goliath, with a subtle slingshot hung over his shoulder. The statue showed us that King David was not a young teen who was a weakling, but instead, he was portrayed as a handsome lad with a very well-built physique and very strong.

So it's true that God anointed King David through the prophet Samuel at a very young age, but what happened immediately after was probably something he was not expecting. Well, nothing much happened. He probably came back to his flock of sheep afterward, and his brothers returned to the battlefield. He probably felt, *Well, I was chosen to become the next king, but so what? What shall I do now?* He received the anointing, but the appointing is far from being realized. His appointing

Usually, when God has anointed you for something, He would make sure you are up for the job. Sometimes He would create a really big situation in your life that will make you more equipped to fulfill your calling.

is yet to come, and I believe it's because God wanted to equip him further. Usually, when God has anointed you for something, He would make sure you are up for the job. Sometimes He would create a really big situation in your life that will make you more equipped to fulfill your calling. Imagine if God made David king immediately after Samuel had chosen him, probably the rest of Israel will not even pay attention or take him seriously. They probably won't see David as a worthy successor to King Saul. God Himself said that man looks at the outward appearance. What had he accomplished at that time? He was only a shepherd who played the lyre. He needed something big to happen in his life. David had to prove something first, and this was for the people whom he would eventually rule over. So remember that when God anoints, He will also help us achieve our best shape to fulfill His calling. In the case of King David, He created not just a big opportunity but also literally a gigantic situation in order to give him the credibility that he needed for the people of Israel to look up to him and respect him as their next king. True enough, one day when he was bringing food to his brothers on the battlefield, God set him up for a very important task. He was about to face his giant, and his life will never be the same from that day on. One of the most notable stories about King David, and if I may use the phrase "catapulted him to stardom" was when he fought this giant warrior from the Philistine army—Goliath.

I think most of us know the story even from elementary school or Sunday school. Three of King David's brothers were fighting the war against the Philistines while the unassuming David went back and forth to the battlefield to bring food to his brothers and at the same time tended the flock for his father. Who would pay attention to a guy who merely brought food to the soldiers of the king's army? King David was practically a nobody compared to the mighty warriors of King Saul. He won't even attract any attention.

There is a good lesson to be learned here. Sometimes, people who are unassuming, down-to-earth, and humble; and the "least likely" are the ones used by God to accomplish extraordinary tasks. This tells us that we should treat people equally. Each person deserves equal treatment and respect from others. I always hear from the older people when I was much younger that life is like a wheel; sometimes you are at the bottom, and sometimes you are on top. Those people whom we think are at the bottom now while we are on top can just be over the top one day, and maybe at that time, we'll be at the bottom.

The Philistines were famous for their advanced and innovative techniques in terms of the use of iron, particularly as a weapon of war. When other kingdoms were still using primitive weapons made of wood, the Philistines were already using iron weapons, and this made the Philistines a real force to reckon with. In most times during Israel's history, the Philistines had always been among the deadly enemies of God's chosen people. In this specific encounter between the Israelites and the Philistines in a place called Valley of Elah, the Philistines paraded their war hero Goliath of Gath. He was a war champion from the camp of the Philistines, and most Bible scholars believe that his height was approximately nine feet nine inches. He was obviously taller than any of the tallest NBA players that we have in our time today. He can easily win most sports competition like basketball, boxing, wrestling, and probably even long jump. He challenged the Israelites for forty days—morning and evening—but nobody was brave enough to fight him. Who would? Fighting this giant was tantamount to committing suicide. Nobody was brave enough to accept the challenge, not even King Saul who was described in the Bible as a tall person. In 1 Samuel 19:2 it says, *"And he was a head taller than anyone else."* But despite his strong physique, King Saul was also afraid to fight Goliath. He may be strong but definitely not strong enough to defeat this giant. The stake was also very high. If the Israelites lose to Goliath, they'll become slaves to the Philistines; therefore, fighting this giant head-on was technically synonymous with surrendering or throwing the white towel on behalf of the whole nation of Israel.

In our lives today, how many times have we thought of just giving up or surrendering to our problems because we are facing a giant? We just want to give up because we are intimidated, and we are overwhelmed by the enormous size of the challenges ahead of us. King David was different. He did not look at the size of his problem but instead focused on the bigness of his God. He was not intimidated by the enormous Goliath, but the greatness of the Good Shepherd inspired him.

To make the long story short, King David, during one of his routine food deliveries to his brothers, heard the challenge made by Goliath to the scared troops of King Saul. To the big surprise of everyone, King David rose up to the challenge. Obviously, no one took him seriously, not Goliath, not his brothers, not the other soldiers, or not even King Saul. They thought he was either crazy or just being too conceited. His brothers also got mad at him, thinking that he was just full of air. I love how King David spoke to the men who were so afraid to face Goliath. He never called him a giant. He never got intimidated by his height. He knew that Goliath was taunting the Sovereign God of the universe, and he knew he needed to do something. He said in 1 Samuel 17:26, *"Who is this uncircumcised Philistine that he should defy the armies of the living God?"* King David may not be as strong as the other soldiers or as tall as Goliath, but he had complete trust in His God that He can deliver him against the giant. He remembered how the Lord delivered him out of the paw of the lion and the bear. We know how the story ended. King David defeated Goliath using a slingshot, and he cut his head in the end with a sword. The defeat of their prize fighter eroded the confidence of the Philistines, and in the end, they lost the battle to the Israelites.

In this story, we can learn how important it is to remember the past victories over what seem to be gigantic challenges that we face, but the Lord has delivered us and enabled us to be victorious. It gives us the confidence to face new trials whenever we remember what the Lord has done for us in the past. King David simply recalled how the Lord delivered him from equally big

> **Remembering past victories allow us to be more confident in our present struggles and even look forward to bigger challenges in the future.**

opponents such as the bear and the lion, and we can just see his confidence in facing battles regardless of how tough the challenges may be. Sometimes when we face a daunting challenge, we act as if it is the end of the world. We lack confidence. We are afraid, and we don't have the courage to move forward nor the strength to face our problems. We either get depressed or feel defeated already even prior to trying anything. We sometimes just tune out and ignore the problem. However, all we need to do is to look back and remember how God has delivered us in our past challenges and difficulties. Remembering past victories allow us to be more confident in our present struggles and even look forward to bigger challenges in the future. King David's courage was also not dependent on his own abilities. He knows that the problem in front of him was big, literally and figuratively. There was also a lot at stake because if he loses the battle with Goliath, the whole army will become subject to the Philistines. The risk was too much, but King Saul did not have much choice—either he allows King David to fight Goliath or just outrightly surrender to the Philistines. In King David's case, he did not let the bigness of his problem frustrate or scare him, but he reminded himself how much bigger God is compared to the giant in front of him. He reminded himself that if God was able to deliver him from wild animals, God can certainly deliver him from Goliath. This was what differentiated King David from the rest of Saul's army at that time. Everyone else saw the bigness of the problem facing them, but David saw the bigness of God.

It reminds me of the twelve spies sent out by Moses to spy on the promised land of Canaan while the Israelites were at Kadesh Barnea. After forty days of exploring the land, the twelve spies returned. Unfortunately, ten out of the twelve spies carried very bad reports. They said that those people who were living in the Promised Land were giants, and they seemed like grasshoppers in their own eyes. The Israelites unfortunately, believed the ten spies, which led to their fear, disobedience, and even rebellious attitudes. Because of this, God allowed them to suffer wandering in the wilderness for forty years. Those ten men who brought the bad report died in the plague. Fortunately, two men believed God's promise; they were Joshua and Caleb. If you were there, would you believe the ten spies? Or would you believe the other two? Are we not usually swayed by the rule of the majority? We always hear "majority rules." That wasn't the case during this time. God already promised them victory. All they needed to do was to go in and take the land. Imagine this was the same God who parted the Red Sea so they can cross on dry land from their Egyptian bondage, and yet they cannot trust Him well enough that He can deliver them from those people occupying the Promised Land. They just had to obey and trust God that He will fulfill His part of the bargain.

A lot of people even during our time today walk by sight and not by faith. The Bible tells us otherwise. Hebrews 11:6 tells us, *"And without faith it is impossible to please God, because anyone who comes to him must believe that he exists and that he rewards those who earnestly seek Him."* God wants us to have a strong faith in Him. Sometimes the people around us see things differently, and they will tell us that we cannot move on and achieve the things that we want to achieve. People sometimes will say to us that we are not good enough, and they can discourage us from moving forward, especially our loved ones; most of them mean well and they have good intentions. However, most of the time, it is only between us and the Lord, and we are the only ones who know the real score. In fact, even our very selves may misunderstand a situation a lot of times. Only God knows what's the real story behind every story. We just have to trust God that He knows what He's doing.

> **Only God knows what's the real story behind every story. We just have to trust God that He knows what He's doing.**

As King David was preparing to face Goliath, there was one point when King Saul wanted David to wear his armor, but David refused to do it. He just wasn't comfortable doing it. He wasn't wired or shaped by God to wear an armor. In fact, to him it was a distraction or a baggage, and he didn't want to rely on any kind of armor or sword made by man. He knew that no matter what he was wearing, it's his big God who can truly deliver him from that dangerous situation. He knew that God will use whatever experience he had in the past to accomplish his task at hand. At that point, he was very skilled in the slingshot, and that's all he needed in order to spoil that victory that would have been easily won by the Philistines.

Have you ever faced a giant? Have you ever fought your Goliath? It can be a major problem, a serious challenge, a sickness or any crisis

> **We have our Good Shepherd who is certainly bigger than any kind of giant that we may ever face in this life.**

that seem so enormous that we are so overwhelmed and intimidated even just by thinking about it. I'm pretty sure you did at some point. There are so many giants that we have to face— giants of anxiety, giants of addiction, giants of sickness, giants of failures, and other things that seem to bring us so low and make us feel so small and insignificant. King David confidently ran toward his giant, not away from it. Our usual tendency when we face our giants was to run away as fast as we could, crawl under the table, duck somewhere because some of us simply don't have the confidence to fight the battle head-on. Just like King David, we must realize that we are not supposed to face our giants alone. We have our Good Shepherd who is undoubtedly bigger than any kind of giant that we may ever face in this life. We should look at the greatness of our God and not the bigness of our problems. We should trust Him enough that He is capable of defeating any of the giants that we might face in our lives. Just like what I mentioned earlier, the battle between David and Goliath involved a test of faith on the part of David and a demonstration of God's supernatural power in front of His people. These huge challenges, trials, or tests are necessary for us to build our faith and make it even stronger. Whenever we are faced with these kinds of gigantic trials, we have the power coming from the Holy Spirit to stand up with full confidence that we can win the victory through our Good Shepherd. James 1:2–4 says, *"Consider it pure joy, my brothers and sisters, whenever you face trials of many kinds, because you know that the testing of your faith produces perseverance. Let perseverance finish its work so that you may be mature and complete, not lacking anything."* These trials that we face and the giants that we conquer are actually for our good, and we should in fact, consider it pure joy whenever we face trials of any kind.

If we fast-forward to the time when King David probably wrote the Twenty-Third Psalm, Bible scholars believe that this was the time when Absalom was chasing him. It was described as the darkest and the most depressing time of King David's life—when he was being pursued by his own son like a fugitive or a wild animal. King David was an accomplished warrior, and I don't think he would mind being pursued by his enemies and I don't think he'll be afraid of anybody. I think he would always welcome these kinds of challenges. But being pursued by his own flesh and blood is a different story. Being pursued by his own son would for sure reminds him time and time again how a failure of a father he was.

A lot of the things happened to King David, particularly the struggles and hardships that he experienced later in his life, and this can be traced back to a particular stage in his life. He committed terrible sins of adultery and murder. One evening, when he was the king of Israel, the Bible aptly describes it in 2 Samuel 11:1, "*In the spring, when kings go off to war,*" he was walking around the roof of the palace, and he saw a beautiful woman bathing. First of all, in those days, wars were fought during springtime. Usually, during winter, the warring nations or tribes would go on a ceasefire because there was no point sacrificing the lives of the soldiers in the midst of a really bad weather. There was obviously something wrong with the picture being painted in the opening verse. It said that during spring, kings go off to war. David was the king; therefore, he should not be wasting his time in the palace, and he should be out there fighting some wars. His able and trustworthy men were out there in the battlefield, fighting and risking their lives. You have probably heard the saying, "An empty mind is the devil's workshop." If we don't keep ourselves busy with the things of God, the enemy will try and tempt us to do certain things that we'll surely regret in the future. Most of the people who fall into the enemy's trap are those people who have more time in their hands to spare. It reminds me of the seminars that my wife and I attended about social media and Internet addiction. Those people who got hooked on pornography are the ones who have more time to surf the Internet. They don't make themselves busy with something else. Same is true in the church. Those members who eventually turn away from the faith are the ones who seldom attend fellowships and Sunday services.

King David had allowed himself to be an open target for the enemy. He would have been better off in the battlefield. He was skilled in the art of war anyway. But staying in the palace when he shouldn't be staying in those times was a clear recipe for disaster and undoubtedly a poor exercise of judgment. True enough, when he saw this triple B (i.e. *beautiful Bathsheba bathing*), he got interested in her, and at that very moment, he gave the devil a foothold in his life. He asked one of his servants about her, and he learned further that this woman, Bathsheba, was the wife of one of his valiant and loyal officers in the army, Uriah, who was at that moment fighting Israel's enemies. He summoned Bathsheba. One thing had led to another, and King David ended up having sexual relations with Bathsheba. When she got pregnant, he recalled Uriah from the battle hoping that he will have sexual relations with his wife while at home, and this could have been the perfect cover-up for his affair. But King David miscalculated one tiny detail. Uriah was an honorable man! He cannot, in his good conscience, do such a thing and sleep with his wife while the whole army whom he was a part of, was fighting for the king and the nation of Israel. Instead of getting convicted and be impressed with the integrity of his military officer, this disappointed King David in his desire to cover up his adulterous acts, instructed his men to put Uriah in front of the battlefield where the fighting was fiercest; and true enough, poor Uriah got killed in battle. King David made the "perfect cover-up," or so he thought. He married Bathsheba, and in the eyes of the kingdom, he was even a generous and kindhearted king who looked after a widow of a soldier who died in battle. He can fool everyone in the kingdom. He can pretend to care and appear holy in front of his subjects, but he cannot fool God. The Good Shepherd knows what's going on in every man's heart. King David himself wrote Psalms 139:1–4, which says, "*You have searched me, Lord, and you know me. You know when I sit and when I rise; you perceive my thoughts from afar. You discern my going out and my lying down; you are familiar with all my ways. Before a word is on my tongue you, Lord, know it completely.*"

Because of this series of sinful events in his life, a few months down the road, he was rebuked by a prophet named Nathan. Instead of immediately confronting him with his sins, Nathan told King David a story. It was about two men, one rich and the other poor. The rich man owned a large number of sheep and cattle, while the poor man only had one little ewe lamb. The poor man loved his little lamb. He took care of it, fed it, and he treated the lamb like his own child. One day a traveler came to the rich man. Instead of taking one of his own sheep to prepare a meal for the traveler, he took the little lamb owned by the poor man. Upon hearing that story, King David burned with anger against that man. He said in 2 Samuel 12:5, *"As surely as the Lord lives, the man who did this must die!"* King David was not expecting that the story Nathan told him was an analogy of what he actually did with Uriah by taking not only the love of his life Bathsheba but also taking his life. Are we not like that sometimes? We are too quick to pronounce judgment if the sin is committed by another person. We are too quick to condemn someone else, but sometimes, we are even worse. We are sometimes committing a more serious sin. If we look ourselves in the mirror, a lot of times we are even worse than the person we are judging or condemning. Jesus said in Matthew 7:5, *"First take the plank out of your own eye, and then you will see clearly to remove the speck from your brother's eye."*

After being rebuked by the prophet Nathan, King David realized how grave and serious were the sins that he had committed. While he had repented of everything and acknowledged the gravity of his sin realizing that his crime was ultimately an offense against the Lord, King David accepted the fact that he cannot escape the consequences of those sins. He knew that the only way for him to learn from these tragic events in his life was by facing the consequences of his wrong decisions. Among these consequences were the shame and hardship caused by the downfall of the kingdom of Israel and the rebellion of his own son Absalom. God was actually merciful enough that he spared King David and even his son King Solomon about the division of Israel into the northern and southern

> Don't we all learn life's best lessons in the midst of pain? Don't we all promise not to commit the same mistakes again but a lot of times we keep on sinning against the Lord?

43

kingdoms. Painful? Yes! Tragic? For sure! But this was the only way King David can learn his lessons.

Don't we all learn life's best lessons in the midst of pain? Don't we all promise not to commit the same mistakes again but a lot of times we keep on sinning against the Lord? It is pretty much like a small kid who has been warned by his parents over and over again not to touch the hot oil lamp, but he kept on coming back until one time he actually touched the lamp and burnt his finger. It hurt him so much. He promised never again will he dare touch the lamp. He learned his lesson the hard way.

King David's life was very colorful. It was painted in different colors in the Scripture without any intention to make him look good nor hide the real truth about his failures. God knows that by showing the life of King David, along with his ups and downs and for what it was, we can all learn from it and understand the fact that God is a God of second chances. He gives people a fair chance to repent. People like King David, who may have committed adultery and murder, have a second chance. We can very well relate to his experience that we do not have to be perfect. We have to be humble enough to admit our mistakes, ask for forgiveness, and change our ways for the better.

God may have brought down King David so low that at certain points in his life, he was like a beggar or a fugitive running away from everything. However, in God's perfect timing, He brought King David up again. Remember that for God to lift us up, He must bring us down first. And for God to make us whole, He needs to make us broken.

God later on, allowed King David to prosper during his remaining time as king of Israel. He also blessed his son King Solomon by giving him extraordinary wisdom and tremendous wealth. Imagine how God has used King David and his descendants, and I think the highest honor that God has bestowed upon King David was the fact that it was through his lineage approximately one thousand years after that the promised Messiah would walk here on earth. If you have read the prophetic books in the Old Testament like the book of Hosea and believe in the future millennial reign of Christ here on earth, King David will reign under Jesus as coregent during the one thousand years millennial kingdom. For sure, it's not over for King David, just like with anyone of us. God is a God of second chances. God is not over with you yet.

Like King David, most of us failed miserably in the past. Like King David, we may have committed some really serious wrongdoings. Can you relate to King David's experience? Have you committed similar mistakes as he did? You look back at your life and you look down on yourself because of all the wrong decisions you made, and you feel that you are not even worthy to look up to God. You feel unworthy of anything because you know you have failed God miserably. I supposed King David felt the same way when he wrote this Psalm. He had full trust and confidence in the Lord that no matter how much problems and disappointments he had caused his family and most especially God in his life, he knew that God was willing to accept him back and bring him to *dwell in His house forever*. I hope and pray that we can have the same trust and confidence in the Lord. God does not look at our imperfections and sins since no one is good enough to meet His standards anyway. All of us are not worthy. No one has sinned bigger or smaller than another person. We have all sinned and fell short of God's glory and righteousness. If we have genuinely surrendered our life to the Good Shepherd, every time God looks at us, He sees not our own righteousness, but also, He sees the righteousness of Jesus in our lives. If there is one thing that I would like my readers to retain and "take home" in this book, that is *a deep longing toward having a personal relationship with Jesus.* If this happens to you while reading this book, and if God uses this book for you to realize that there is something or actually someone missing in your life, and that is Jesus Christ, I can say I already received my reward, and I give God the full glory He deserves. Toward the end of this book, I added a section called *Invitation.* In this chapter, I have discussed a great deal about how you can have a personal and intimate relationship with Jesus Christ by making Him your Good Shepherd. Like King David, my prayer is that each one of us may be called by God "a man (or woman) after His own heart!"

Reflection Questions

1. Is there someone in your life that you look up to? This person may have had a great influence on you while growing up. Or this person could be your role model in many areas such as career, family, or even stability in life.
2. What would happen if you learn something negative about this person's life or character? Or what if this person offends you directly? Will you give this person a second chance to make amends? Will your picture of this person change?
3. Have you experienced facing a formidable opponent in life? A really tough situation or problem of gigantic proportion? How did you handle it?

The Twenty-Third Psalm

A psalm of King David.

> The Lord is my shepherd, I lack nothing.
> He makes me lie down in green pastures,
> he leads me beside quiet waters,
> he refreshes my soul.
> He guides me along the right paths
> for his name's sake.
> Even though I walk
> through the darkest valley,
> I will fear no evil,
> for you are with me;
> your rod and your staff,
> they comfort me.
> You prepare a table before me
> in the presence of my enemies.
> You anoint my head with oil;
> my cup overflows.
> Surely your goodness and love will follow me
> all the days of my life,
> and I will dwell in the house of the Lord
> forever.
> (New International Version)

For comparison purposes, as a lot of people may be more familiar with a different version, I am also including here the NASB or New American Standard Bible version of the Twenty-Third Psalm.

The following chapters are also divided according to this version of the Twenty-Third Psalm.

> The Lord is my shepherd, I shall not want.
> He makes me lie down in green pastures;
> He leads me beside quiet waters.
> He restores my soul;
> He guides me in the paths of righteousness
> For His name's sake.
> Even though I walk through the valley of the shadow of death,
> I fear no evil, for You are with me;
> Your rod and Your staff, they comfort me.
> You prepare a table before me in the presence of my enemies;
> You have anointed my head with oil;
> My cup overflows.
> Surely goodness and lovingkindness will follow me all the days of my life,
> And I will dwell in the house of the Lord forever.

The Good Shepherd and His Sheep

The Lord is my shepherd.

—Psalm 23:1a

The Bible uses different analogies to describe God's relationship over His creation. The most popular and most commonly used among these analogies is God as our Abba Father. God wants us to have an intimate kind of relationship with Him that closely resembles that of a father to his children. We also referred to God as our Savior because we know that through His Son Jesus Christ, we have been saved from eternal death caused by our sins. We call God our Lord, the Almighty, our Banner, our Provider, the Great I Am, and a lot of other names and references. One of the reasons why I chose the Twenty-Third Psalm to reflect upon as my first book is because I believe one of the best metaphors used in the Bible to describe the Lord concerning His relationship with us is being our *Shepherd.* Jesus calls Himself our Good Shepherd, and in the first four lines of the Twenty-Third Psalm, the Lord is compared by King David to a shepherd. What makes this comparison very interesting is that it does not only fittingly describe the Lord as the Shepherd in terms of how He treats us but it also aptly describes God's children, presupposing they follow Him as His "sheep." A lot of people will probably dislike this statement, but at this point, it is very important to note the reality that not all people in this world are God's children, or metaphorically, not everyone in this world is His

> **While everyone is created by God and God loves His creation, not everyone is considered to be part of His family. Not everyone is considered His sheep.**

sheep. While everyone is created by God and God loves His creation, not everyone is considered to be part of His family. Not everyone is considered His sheep. In the same manner, not everyone in this world recognizes God as his or her Shepherd or as his or her father. Some people have purposely rejected God in their lives. Some people have blasphemed God either directly or indirectly, and for centuries, they have persecuted those who are faithfully practicing their faith, and they have made a mockery of the sacrifices of Jesus Christ on the cross. There are other flocks who follow a different shepherd or master, and while this is unfortunate, it is a reality. In fact, Jesus said there will be more people who will choose not to follow Him. There are a lot of good people here in this world. A lot of them are our friends and even family members. There are also a lot of sincere people around us. However, the important reality that we have to face is that being good and being sincere is not enough. We have to be sincerely correct when it comes to our relationship with God. Jesus said in John 4:24, *"God is spirit, and his worshipers must worship in the spirit and in truth."* It's not enough that we sincerely believe in something, and we experience a great deal of emotions on that belief, but it is imperative that our belief is anchored on something we can totally rely on. God wants us to worship Him in spirit and in truth. Our faith in God must be strongly based on the Scriptures. I will allow a great deal of discussion about this in the chapter, "What Profit Is a Man."

At this point, let us clarify and have a better understanding of these two metaphors: Jesus Christ is the Shepherd, and those who believe in Him as their Lord and Savior are His sheep. King David used this excellent metaphor of calling God as his shepherd in the first verse of the Twenty-Third Psalm.

Another interesting thought in the opening verses of this psalm is the fact that King David knew what he was talking about. He was clearly speaking from his own experience, so he's got credibility. King David was a shepherd himself after all in his younger years, and we can say he was a very good shepherd, so he knew what he was talking about. It would be an oxymoron to say that he is a hands-on shepherd because a true shepherd needs to be hands on. He wrote this Psalm not just out of theoretical ideas or know-how but mainly from his own experience of actually tending his father's sheep. In ancient Israel, a typical shepherd is not necessarily that charming, romantic, and muscular nomad that you will see roaming around with his flock from one place to another. Shepherds are usually dirty, severely tanned, and they don't smell good. Shepherds are a common profession in ancient Israel, and they are pretty much like the farmers in our time today or even construction workers. It's a blue-collar job, and it's not something most people were looking forward to becoming one. They don't wear neckties or business suits. They don't drive fancy cars or trucks, and being a shepherd is not a high-paying job. But despite all of these, being a shepherd is a serious responsibility. Sometimes, the shepherd's life gets endangered. The Bible tells us that in order to protect his sheep, the shepherd had to fight with predators like foxes, lions, and bears.

In the opening verse of the Twenty-Third Psalm, King David called the Lord as "my Shepherd." He did not say the Lord is "our Shepherd" or the Lord is the "Shepherd of all people," but instead he used the pronoun *my*, and to me, this only indicates one thing: King David is very much secured in his faith, and he is certain and absolutely confident about his personal relationship with the Lord. He had this intimacy with God, and King David knew in his heart that this God knows him personally as well, and he was calling up to a God who is capable of having a personal and intimate relationship with him. This is a very important reflection that I would like for every reader of this book to understand. Each one of us has to have that personal and intimate relationship with our Maker. It doesn't matter who we are or what we have done in our lives; we just need to realize that God desires to establish that personal relationship with each one of us.

> It doesn't matter who we are or what we have done in our lives; we just need to realize that God desires to establish that personal relationship with each one of us.

If King David calls God his shepherd, what does it make him? A sheep, of course! King David, the "earthly" shepherd, is now acknowledging the fact that as far as his relationship with the Heavenly God is concerned, he is now the sheep, and God is his Good Shepherd. The Bible tells us that the shepherd King David who was very experienced and was able to defeat ferocious animals like foxes, bear, and lion, he is now humbling down and considering himself to be a sheep of his Good Shepherd. This is a clear demonstration of humility in his attitude as he knows his standing before a holy and magnificent God. No wonder the Bible calls him a "Man After God's Own Heart." This is one of the reasons why I like the story of King David. He has achieved a lot in his life, and his feats are unparalleled by any other king in Israel's history. Can you imagine becoming a great warrior and eventually becoming a king of a nation? He was wealthy. He had power, and he had all the material things that anybody could have wished for during that time. He was even blessed with amazing skills in music. He played musical instruments and wrote psalms, and yet, he willingly bowed himself to the Lord recognizing His sovereignty over him as his Shepherd. Yes, he was an amazing warrior, and his leadership skills are impeccable, but he has a humble, obedient heart and a godly attitude.

Aside from the Twenty-Third Psalm, there are more than seventy verses in the Scripture that use the metaphor "shepherd" to represent God. I will only list five scriptural references in this book to show how much God wanted to stress out to each one of us that He is our Good Shepherd:

> *He tends his flock like a shepherd: He gathers the lambs in his arms and carries them close to his heart; he gently leads those that have young. (Is. 40:11)*
>
> *Hear us, Shepherd of Israel, you who lead Joseph like a flock. You who sit enthroned between the cherubim shine forth. (Ps. 80:1)*
>
> *Now may the God of peace, who through the blood of the eternal covenant brought back from the dead our Lord Jesus, that great Shepherd of the sheep. (Heb. 13:20)*

For you were like sheep going astray, but now you have returned to the Shepherd and Overseer of your souls. (1 Pet. 2:25)

Chapter 10 of John, which I will further elaborate at the end of this book.

From the above passages, the Scripture is pretty consistent in using the shepherd analogy when referring to God. The word *shepherd* comes from the Hebrew word *ra`ah* and in Greek *poimen,* which means a herdsman or someone who pastures, tends, grazes, and takes care of a flock of sheep. While we all know that there can be no perfect analogy fitting to be used to describe God, comparing Him to a shepherd is probably one of the two closest analogies we can use, the other one by calling Him our Abba Father. God uses these two analogies Himself. Being a shepherd during biblical times is probably one of the most humble and difficult professions you can ever become. In fact, it is not what we consider a wealthy profession. If you are a shepherd, you are most likely one of the poorest people in the community. However, we know that the Bible tells us that God opposes the proud but gives grace to the humble. God came to this earth in human form as a humble baby in a manger wrapped in swaddling clothes, and do you know whom the angels announced Jesus Christ's coming first and foremost? The angels announced Christ's birth to the lowly shepherds in Bethlehem. This tells us how God looks at the humble and simple people on Earth, and God does not mind if we compare Him to a humble person like a shepherd. God specializes in raising up people who are humble and lowly. Jesus said in Matthew 23:12, *"For those who exalt themselves will be humbled, and those who humble themselves will be exalted."* What is important for us to understand is not the social standing of being a shepherd that matters but the kind of attitude that a good shepherd has towards his flock. This kind of mentality is what speaks more about God's character and nature! He wants us to understand the personal and intimate relationship that He wants to have with each one of us by simply looking at the typical example of a shepherd. A lot of times, God, in spite of His supreme know-how and intelligence, uses words all over the Scripture to describe relationships that we can easily understand. God knows that if He uses the analogy of a shepherd to describe His relationship with us, we can easily get the picture. We won't have a hard time understanding how an unseen God can relate to us on a daily basis as a shepherd. We don't need a theology degree to understand the message that He wants to get across. Comparing Himself to a shepherd is something that even somebody with a very limited education can easily comprehend, and we definitely cannot make an excuse telling God that we can't figure out the kind of relationship that He wants to establish with each one of us. It's quite simple and straightforward: God wants us to recognize Him as our Good Shepherd.

I personally have some experience growing on a farm; however, I cannot say I know a lot of things about being a shepherd. In our farm, I have seen some herdsmen who did not really tend a flock of sheep but mostly cows or carabaos, but there is a lot of similarity in the way these herdsmen take care of their flock in comparison with the shepherds in the Middle East or North America. Like shepherds, the farmers that I knew of when I was young surely had intimate relationships with their farm animals. Like a good and caring shepherd, they call each one of their farm animals by name. A good shepherd knows his flock very well—which one is strong, which one is weak, which one needs the most help, which one is the smartest and even the one who normally strays away or has the tendency to leave the flock whenever possible. He knows their strengths and weaknesses. He knows which one can be easily lured by another shepherd, thereby straying from the flock. He knows which ones are stubborn and the high-maintenance ones. I remember when I was small, my father bought a carabao, and we named her Bakekang. A carabao is a very popular farm animal in the Philippines. It is a swamp-type domestic water buffalo and is considered as the national animal of the Philippines. She was a very lazy carabao. All she wanted to do was to eat and sleep. She wasn't really much of a help in our farm, but we nevertheless treated her well. I remember there was a time she didn't even want to walk, and the only way for her to start walking was when my father tied some grass on her horns and she will just keep on walking trying to catch those grass tied up to her horns because she wanted to eat them. I can say Bakekang was a high-maintenance animal, and it took a lot of effort and patience to take care of her, but my father loved this carabao very much. He bathed her, fed her, and didn't force her to work hard in the farm even if insects kept flying around her head. We rode on her back time and again, and she became like part of our family, more like a pet rather than a work animal. She was more of a symbol in our farm because all the farmers have carabaos as well, but my dad used his farm tractor to till the land most of the time.

A good shepherd knows what the strengths and weaknesses of his flock. He knows which one has a weak leg or which one has the strong one. He knows which one has poor hearing, which one eats a lot, and which one is usually sick. Likewise, shepherds also know their flock's enemy. In the ancient Middle East, there were lots of ferocious wolves and even lions or bears who were always out there waiting for an opportunity to devour someone from the flock. This is the same analogy used in the Bible, which compares our enemy, the devil, to a roaring lion, who is always out there waiting for someone he can devour. A good shepherd can tell if an enemy is waiting for his flock out there. Shepherds have to be always alert and should be able to keep a keen eye to make sure that there is no danger lurking ahead.

> **If we spend more and more time with God, in prayer, in understanding His word and putting those words into practice, we become more and more like Him.**

Good shepherds also smell alike with his flock. People think this was a joke, but there is a logical explanation why a shepherd would smell like his sheep. This tells us that a really good shepherd spends a great deal of time being together with his flock to the point that they smell alike. He bathes his flock or bathes with his flock, and sometimes he had to sleep with his flock especially if he can sense that there is potential danger waiting. Sometimes when the shepherd brings his flock to a grazing place, it won't be safe anymore for them to go home, so they will just spend the night in the wilderness. Isn't God like that to each one of us? We are created in His image. The

Bible says in Genesis 1:27, *"So God created mankind in his own image, in the image of God he created them; male and female he created them."* God protects us, and He spends time with us, and most especially, He knows our enemy very well. He provides all we need, and He convicts our hearts once He sees that we are slowly giving away to the temptations of this world. If we spend more and more time with God, in prayer, in understanding His word and putting those words into practice, we become more and more like Him. One of our purposes here on Earth is to become more and more like Jesus. To put it in the same analogy, the more we spend time with Jesus, we "smell" more and more like Him and we become more and more godly in our character. The apostle Paul has a very interesting command in his letter to the Philippians. It says in Philippians 2:5–11:

> *In your relationships with one another, have the same mindset as Christ Jesus: Who, being in very nature God, did not consider equality with God something to be used to his own advantage; rather, he made himself nothing by taking the very nature of a servant, being made in human likeness. And being found in appearance as a man, he humbled himself by becoming obedient to death—even death on a cross! Therefore God exalted him to the highest place and gave him the name that is above every name, that at the name of Jesus every knee should bow, in heaven and on earth and under the earth, and every tongue acknowledge that Jesus Christ is Lord, to the glory of God the Father.*

God wants us to be like Jesus. He wants us to emulate His humility, His compassion, and His love for others. It is a funny analogy to say that the shepherd and his sheep smell alike, but if you will relate this analogy with our Christian life, it makes a lot of sense. People will know that we are real followers of Christ if we become more and more like Him. People should see in the way we live our lives the humility, compassion, and love of Christ. Even those people who don't know Jesus can't help but wonder the godly character that they can see in us. They will start asking. Why are we not retaliating when being wronged? Why are we so caring and loving to others? Why are we so concerned about others' well-being? As other people get more and more curious about us, it becomes a springboard, a good platform to introduce our Lord Jesus Christ to them. We tell them that we are like this because of our Lord, because of our Good Shepherd.

Now before we even continue talking about God as our Shepherd, there is an inevitable resulting analogy in calling God as our Shepherd: calling Him "shepherd" makes us His sheep! Just like King David, if we have surrendered our lives to God, that makes us His sheep, or that makes us part of His flock. We become His family. I would like to spend a great deal of time discussing our condition as God's sheep or as part of God's flock. The Bible has mentioned this several times calling all those who believe in Him to be His sheep and to be part of His flock.

First of all, God calls us sheep not because of what we can or cannot do. He doesn't call us His sheep because of who we are or what we have. We are not part of His flock certainly not because we are cute, bubbly, or cuddly. Sometimes, we get a picture of a sheep as a stuffed toy, which is huggable, soft, innocent, and harmless. God does not call us His sheep because we have impressive credentials or maybe from a sheep's perspective because we produce the finest wool. It's not about our abilities or our gifts, skills, or talents. No. God does not call us "sheep" because we are obedient, tame, or down-to-earth. We are not called "sheep" because we are easy to get along with or because we are homebodies or domesticated. We are not called "sheep" because we are patient or submissive. Sorry to disappoint you, but we are not called by God at all to be part of His flock because of "us," but it is simply and solely because of His own grace. He chose us to be part of His flock because He wants to. The faith we have to open our hearts and receive Jesus in our lives is a gift from God because of His grace and mercy.

I believe God calls us "sheep" simply because we are dumb! Well, obviously compared against the wisdom of God, we are dumb for sure and there is nothing we can do about that. We may think we're smart beings because maybe some of us have attained a very high level of education. We have our master's and even doctor's degrees, but we always fall short of God's wisdom. There is nothing that we already know and will know that God does not know. The Bible says in 1 Corinthians 3:19, *"For the wisdom of this world is foolishness in God's sight."* Have you ever seen a sheep performing smart acts at a circus festival? Have you ever seen a sheep doing some impressive tricks during town festivities? Not really, right? Have you ever seen a sheep trainer pretty much like a lion tamer or a dog-trick master? Nope, I have not met even one person. It is not a common sight. In fact, I have never seen something like it. You do not see a sheep, upon the command of his master, would lie down, roll, fetch, or dance. You do not see these things because the sheep, generally speaking, is a dumb animal. They are not capable of being trained to do all these tricks. They are not wired by our Creator to do those things. The sheep are not even good at taking care of themselves, and God knows that we are not good at taking care of ourselves either. A lot of times, we knowingly or unknowingly harm ourselves. We do things that we think is good for us, but in the end, it gets us into trouble. We definitely need a Shepherd to be with us. We definitely need someone to look after us and take care of our needs. We are not capable of really taking care of ourselves. Oftentimes, we don't even know what is good for us. We try to figure out what we need and find the answers to our questions, but we end up getting those answers from the wrong sources. If God leaves us on our own even for a second, everything will be a disaster. We need to be always connected to the Source of everything, our Good Shepherd. If God stops looking after us, we'll even die because He is the source of our very own life. Recognizing this fact should give us an attitude of humility. We are dumb. We become a truly wise person if we have Jesus in our lives. The book of Proverbs has mentioned this so many times. A person who has no God in his life is a fool and nothing else. King David himself wrote in Psalm 14:1, *"The fool says in his heart, "There is no God."*

I met a shepherd once, and he told me that the sheep do not have a keen sense of smell. Sometimes they will just eat poisonous weeds and die. They cannot distinguish which kind of food will be detrimental or harmful to them. That is not so dumb really if you ask me, especially if the sheep don't know that the weeds are poisonous. But you know what I learned is that even if the sheep are dropping dead around the others from eating the poisonous weeds, the other sheep shall continue to eat these toxic weeds until they all die. Now that's dumb. It will not even alarm them even if the other sheep in the flock are dying one by one.

I also believe God calls us sheep because we are simply helpless and defenseless. Jesus said, *"Apart from me you are nothing"* (John 15:15). Sheep are vulnerable animals. They have no fangs, no sharp claws. They can't bite you. They can't outrun you, and they have very little ambition in life. They are not aggressive, and you'll never see sheep in racetracks. I don't remember ever seeing sheep races or a sports team using the sheep as their team mascot. Almost all animals that I have observed has probably at least one outstanding defense mechanism to protect them from predators. Bulls have horns, birds have claws, other animals have fangs, but sheep don't have anything outstanding with them. Their only defense mechanism is they are gregarious animals. The word *gregarious* means they like to band together. This attitude protects them from predators too. Sheep like to get together, and their strength is by being in a flock. They know that if one sheep goes astray, this sheep can get into a lot of trouble. Pretty much like Christians. We love to fellowship together, and this is our strength. The Bible says in Ecclesiastes 4:9–10, *"Two are better than one, because they have a good return for their labor: If either of them falls down, one can help the other up."* King David also wrote in Psalm 133:1, *"How good and pleasant it is when God's people live together in unity!"* A lot of times, when a person stays away from church fellowship, he or she gets easily tempted by the enemy to do certain things that disappoint the Good Shepherd. He or she can be easily lured by the enemy to commit sins and fall into temptations.

Sheep also get easily frightened and confused. Sometimes, in panic, they will just dive blindly toward a precipice or a cliff. Now, this doesn't sound really smart. When enemies like foxes or coyotes attack, the sheep will run around in panic especially if the shepherd is not around. They can be easily harmed by their enemies because they are not the type who will fight back. This reminds me of what Jesus said in Luke 6:29, *"If someone slaps you on one cheek, turn to them the other also."* Jesus is basically saying we just lift up everything to the Good Shepherd as He will always be there to vindicate us when we are abused or taken advantage of. Just like the sheep, we can also get easily frightened and confused. Especially in life-or-death situations or trying moments, sometimes we get confused on which action to take. We sought the advice of people from around us, and a lot of times, we don't know which advice to follow. If we are familiar with the voice of our Good Shepherd, if we read His word and communicate with Him in prayer, I am pretty sure that we shall hear from Him.

Sheep are dirty and untidy animals. They are, by nature, unclean. A cat, dog, or bird can clean itself. Other animals lick, bathe themselves, or roll in the grass to clean themselves but not the sheep! They can get dirty and stinky, and they just stay that way. They will remain filthy indefinitely until the shepherd cleans them or gives them a bath. If the shepherd doesn't pay attention to their wool and clip the wool out from around their eyes, they will get eye infections from all of the filth carried in their wool, and the sheep won't be able to see. They are not capable of cleaning themselves. Just like the sheep, we are also filthy in our own ways. We commit sins and make mistakes, and we are not capable of cleaning ourselves. We need our Good Shepherd to clean us, and He does so because we are cleansed by His blood. He assures us that if we come to Him and ask for forgiveness, He will forgive us. The Apostle Paul wrote to the Ephesians, *"In him we have redemption through his blood, the forgiveness of sins, in accordance with the riches of God's grace"* (Ephesians 1:7).

> **Just like the sheep, we are also filthy in our own ways. We commit sins and make mistakes, and we are not capable of cleaning ourselves.**

Sheep are very dependent beings. They are defenseless, and they are not abundantly endowed with intelligence and lack the capacity to find food and water for themselves in their surroundings. They mainly depend on others to fend for them. If they are going to survive, they need not just a protector but a provider as well. A shepherd to the sheep is both a protector and a provider. Jesus wants us to depend on Him. He wants us to trust Him for every decision and action that we ever take in our lives. Proverbs 3:5–6 tells us, *"Trust in the Lord with all your heart and lean not on your own understanding; in all your ways submit to him, and he will make your paths straight."*

I also read somewhere that a sheep cannot just lie down because a sheep that lies down on his back cannot just easily get up on its own. The sheep need to be helped out by the shepherd so they can get back on their feet. And before they lie down, they must be free of all fear. Sheep will not lie down if they are too close to the other sheep in the same flock, as if they are rubbing on each other. They like to keep a distance from each other especially when they sleep. If tormented by insects like flies or other parasites, the sheep will not lie down, and if they are hungry, the sheep will also not lie down. But look at this, the good shepherd makes the sheep lie down in green pastures as the shepherd gives the sheep rest. That after a long travel or an arduous journey, a good shepherd brings his flock into a place of rest, a place of abundance, the green pasture. In our respective journeys in this life, God is the only one who can provide us true rest and security to make us lie down and feel safe. The Good Shepherd does all those things to His sheep. He gives them security and safety.

> In our respective journeys in this life, God is the only one who can provide us true rest and true security to make us lie down and feel safe.

So to summarize the characteristics of sheep, remember the four *D*s—dumb, dirty, dependent, and defenseless. A male sheep is called a ram. This is basically what was caught up in thickets when Abraham was about to sacrifice Isaac at Mount Moriah. This is found in Genesis 22:13, *"Abraham looked up and there in a thicket he saw a ram caught by its horns. He went over and took the ram and sacrificed it as a burnt offering instead of his son."* A female sheep is called a ewe. The young sheep, on the other hand, is called a lamb. The sheep produce wool, which is taken from their skin follicles. So whenever the Bible calls us sheep, I really don't think it's a compliment because of the four *D*s that I have mentioned earlier.

Here is one thing I want you to remember: whenever we are called sheep, the compliment is really not on us but on the Shepherd. What is important is how much the sheep can accomplish because he has Good Shepherd. The relationship between the shepherd and the sheep works primarily because of the Shepherd. It's not much on what the sheep can do, but it's all about what the Good Shepherd has already done for His sheep.

Like a sheep, we can visit greener pastures because our Good Shepherd leads us there, and everything that we can accomplish in this life is because of Him. It's funny because, at some point, the Lord Jesus Christ describes Himself as a sheep, or to be more specific, as a lamb. In the Gospel of John 1:29, Jesus describes Himself (through John the Baptist calling Him) as *"the Lamb of God, who takes away the sin of the world!"* He did not describe Himself as a lamb because of the same reasons I have described above. He described Himself as a Lamb not because He is defenseless or helpless or dumb but in the area of being the ultimate sacrifice for all mankind. This is very significant because the Israelites were specifically commanded by the Lord to offer an unblemished male lamb without defect in Exodus 12. This kind of sacrifice typifies the final sacrifice that Jesus Christ voluntarily took more than two thousand years ago. Indeed, He is our blameless Lamb who takes away the sins of the world. He is the living sacrifice who redeems us from our sins, and nobody can take His place because we all sinned and fell short of God's glory.

I know you are getting less and less inspired with our description of the sheep, which represents us. This is because there is really nothing inspiring about it. I believe it is important for us to talk more about the Good Shepherd (God) rather than the sheep (ourselves). Looking at the role of the Good Shepherd in our lives, we can now look at ourselves differently. We look at ourselves from the perspective of our Lord. We can start to give ourselves the right value and the right qualification, and that is being the sheep of the Most High God.

The Good Shepherd is obviously very important in the life of King David as he started the Twenty-Third Psalm with the acknowledgment that the Lord is his Shepherd.

Let's talk about the shepherd, which is probably one of the oldest professions. If you have lived in Israel during biblical times, you would see shepherds and sheep all the time. The shepherd takes care of his flock, and he raised them. We know that the sheep has four *D* (dumb, dirty, dependent, and defenseless) qualities, and the role of the shepherd in a sheep's life is beyond measure. The shepherd protects them from their predators and provides for everything the sheep needs. The shepherd usually leads the flock and takes them out on the fields so they can graze (or eat grass and forbs). He usually walks in the front. Since the sheep have a poor eyesight, the sheep rely on the voice of the shepherd, usually a whistle. Israel was mostly desert, so it's not easy for the shepherd to find a place where the flock can eat. There are several flocks of sheep in the desert, so it is important for the sheep to know the shepherd's voice. Otherwise, he might follow another shepherd. They can easily mix up with another flock or another sheep to be mixed up with their flock. The sheep follow the shepherd, and the flock is familiar with the shepherd's voice. Sometimes, in trying to find a place where they could settle, they had to sleep in the desert along with other flocks and other shepherds. So the sheep and shepherd stay together, sleep together, so naturally, they smell alike, they wake up together early so they can be the first to drink water and visit a green pasture. Those who cheat, they just lead and the sheep still follow. Sometimes they imitate the voice of the shepherd so the sheep would follow him. If the sheep know the voice of their shepherd, they won't be misled by the fake shepherds. These counterfeit shepherds imitate the whistle of the true shepherd. Their only intention is to steal, kill, and destroy the flock. A shepherd would usually have two primary tools—his rod and his staff. I have devoted an entire chapter in this book to discuss in detail the metaphor used by King David for rod and staff.

As I have mentioned earlier, the shepherd also communicates to his sheep using his voice, oftentimes in the form of a whistle. A sheep who does not recognize the voice of its shepherd is a good candidate for destruction. When a shepherd whistles, the sheep must recognize it and must act accordingly. Sometimes, the shepherd announces that there is a lurking danger, so the sheep must know and must be very familiar with the voice and whistle of its master. Similarly, if we do not know the voice of God, we are bound for destruction. If we are not familiar with His words, we'll be astray. We might find ourselves joining another flock. We can be separated from our own flock. In our lives today, how do you know the voice of God? How do you know the voice of your Shepherd? We know God's voice through the Bible. We know His words through the scripture that we read because His words are true, His words are timeless, and His words are inerrant. Isaiah 40:8 tells us, *"The grass withers and the flowers fall, but the word of our God endures forever."* The voice of God is in the Bible. The voice of our Shepherd is timeless. It will outlast any kind of life here on Earth. The word of God in the Bible gives us the truth and principles to live by even during our time today. We must search the pages of the Bible because, from this book, we can find the wisest of counsel as we encounter different situations in our lifetime. The reason why a lot of people, a lot of Christians, are being misled by fake shepherds is that they are not familiar with His voice; they do not know the sound of His words. If you spend so much time with someone, that someone becomes very familiar to you—his smell, his mannerisms, his voice and everything about him. If you do not spend enough time with the Lord, obviously, you will not intimately know Him, and you can easily be misled by somebody who is very charismatic but actually teaches wrong doctrines and even lies about God.

So the Lord is likened to a shepherd. By recognizing God as our Good Shepherd, I know it gives us a more vivid and understandable description of His role in our lives. I know that it's human nature to always want to control our lives or even our own destiny. We don't want anybody meddling in our affairs. A lot of people do not recognize the role of God as their Shepherd. They like to do things on their own and don't submit to the lordship of the Shepherd. The problem is not just submission, but we want a particular kind of freedom from God to do things the way we want it and decide on how we will do it. We don't want to be controlled by someone else. This is one of the reasons why the Christian religion is not very attractive to some people. They view Christianity as something with a lot of rules, "ifs" and "buts," a lot of things that you can or cannot do.

In our lives today, who else is likened to a shepherd? Do you know where the word *pastor* came from? It comes from the Greek word *poimēn*, which means shepherd. So a pastor is expected to take care of the Lord's flock. And as a body of believers, like sheep, we should smell alike (I don't think you like the idea, but you know what I mean). The sheep must know and be very familiar with its shepherd and vice versa. The pastor is God's extension to the church, and he plays a similar role with a shepherd in a local church context. He is expected to guide the flock, serve the flock, protect the flock, and lead the flock beside quiet waters. I know it's a very big responsibility to be a pastor. It takes one to know one. If you are a pastor and is reading this book, you must understand the depth of responsibility being placed on your shoulders the moment God called you to shepherd His flock. There is no such person as a perfect pastor as we are ordinary people called upon by an extraordinary God. Although a pastor is a shepherd to his congregation, he is still as sheep to his Good Shepherd. He becomes an effective minister only if his relationship with the Good Shepherd is intimate, authentic, and personal.

Over the years, the church, the body of Christ or God's children, has been rocked by different scandals coming from the very top level of the church hierarchy. We have heard this in the news not just once but several times. It is sad that there are shepherds who are not faithful to their calling, and all they do is to lead their flock astray. The Bible wants these kinds of church leaders to know that there is a much bigger expectation if you are leading a church. James 3:1 says, *"Not many of you should become teachers, my fellow believers, because you know that we who teach will be judged more strictly."* Every follower of Christ, whether a church leader or a simple churchgoer, is expected to exhibit godliness and holiness at all times as they represent God Almighty. We can probably spend so much time sharing the Bible to other people and talking about Christ and His Gospel, but if these people don't see Christ in us, if they don't see us first loving each other within the church, they will not even listen to what we say. The first Bible that they will read is our lives. Are we practicing what we preach? Are we loving each other within the flock?

Are we sharing each other's burden and doing good things to one another? John 13:35 tells us, *"By this everyone will know that you are my disciples, if you love one another."* We can be an effective bearer of the good news of the Gospel if we are showing that we are a part of God's wonderful flock and we have genuine interest and concern to invite others to join our flock as well.

The shepherd and sheep metaphor is a profound mystery. It stresses the pivotal role that the Shepherd plays in the life of His flock. Without Him, the flock will amount to nothing. It expresses the selfless attitude of the Shepherd that He will do anything to protect His sheep. Jesus Christ is our Good Shepherd. He is the Shepherd of our soul. On the other hand, the sheep metaphor tells us how dependent we are and how important for us to rely solely on the Shepherd. We have to realize that we can accomplish nothing apart from Him. We have to recognize that our lives as sheep can only have meaning if truly offered for the glory of the Good Shepherd.

> **We have to realize that our lives as sheep can only have meaning if truly offered for the glory of the Good Shepherd.**

Come to think of it, the sacrifice of the Shepherd in order to protect the lives of His sheep is not only metaphorical. Jesus, our Good Shepherd, literally died for us, His sheep. He walked here on earth and faced all kinds of dangers that each of us could have faced as a result of our sins and shortcomings. But our Good Shepherd took all the beatings for us. The Good Shepherd takes the ultimate sacrifice to express His love for His flock by dying on the cross in order for us to be free from the bondage and punishment of sin. It is so amazing to finally realize this truth. Jesus is indeed our Good Shepherd. Without Him, we were heading straight to the deep ravine of eternal doom. Sometimes I wonder and ponder upon, what have I done for Christ to do all these things for me? The answer is nothing! It is all purely by His grace. It is solely because of His love and mercy. With this mindset, we must live our lives with an attitude of gratitude, forever thanking God for being our Good Shepherd and for making us His sheep.

Reflection Questions

1. What other kinds of analogies would you compare the relationship of God to those who follow Him?
2. Using these analogies, describe the characteristics of both God and yourself (under the assumption that you are a follower of God).
3. Does the definition of a Good Shepherd capture your idea about God's nature? If yes, why? If no, why not?

Jehovah Jireh: God Is Our Provider

I shall not want.

—Psalm 23:1b

I think one of the most difficult challenges a man will ever face throughout his life here on earth is the idea of finding contentment. Contentment is like the fountain of youth or a pot of gold being searched by man for generations, but it has been very elusive, and man cannot find it. It is not because contentment is like a slippery eel or that contentment does not actually exist that is why it has become almost impossible to find. I think the reason is that man is simply looking at the wrong place, and his quest usually heads towards the wrong direction. How many times we tried looking for things, but no matter how much effort we put in, we can't find it because we're looking at the wrong place? Man tried different ways and different approaches hoping that he can find contentment and be satisfied with whatever he accomplishes in life, but there is actually no real contentment apart from the Good Shepherd and from what He can provide. Man, in his own selfish ways, can never find real satisfaction on his own, and it will always dodge him no matter how much he tries. As I get older, my eyes are getting more and more difficult to manage so I had to go to an eye doctor, and he prescribed that I start wearing reading glasses. A couple of times, I thought I lost my reading glasses, and I would spend time looking at them only to find out I was actually wearing them. Sometimes they are just on my head. Contentment is like that. It is not far out there, but it is basically within our reach as it springs out from our heart and our relationship with the Good Shepherd, but we can't find it because we are looking far ahead. Our eyes are fully engaged by the things that we can see from a distance not realizing that contentment is something beyond what is material or physical or visible, but it is very much reachable. Not only that we cannot find contentment on what we achieve, but in fact, we are not capable of doing anything truly good and most especially godly, apart from God. We need to be connected to the Vine, the Source of everything, and the originator of contentment. We need to be in constant communion with the Good Shepherd for us to fully appreciate everything that He has provided us. Then and only then that we can be contented and satisfied with what we have achieved in life. Then and only then that we can bear eternal fruit and be a consistent channel of blessings. God blesses us in order for us to bless others. Blessing others is like bearing fruit. Our Lord Jesus Christ said in John 15:5, *"I am the vine; you are the branches. If you remain in me and I in you, you will bear much fruit; apart from me you can do nothing."*

It is amazing how King David opened the Twenty-Third Psalm focusing on God, his Shepherd. He knew how to start this psalm right. He knew that if he did otherwise, he will not be able to bring glory to his Shepherd, but instead, he might face the tendency of being caught up with his own personal issues rather than praising God and be a blessing to others who will read his psalm. It is worthy to take note that he wrote the Twenty-Third Psalm by starting with God and not focusing on other things like his own personal needs and wants. Did you notice that he did not say "our Shepherd" or "your Shepherd" but instead he wrote, "the Lord is MY Shepherd?" We don't usually make use of the pronoun "my" if we are not certain that we truly have that kind of personal connection. We don't say "my wife, or my children, or my house, or my property" if we are not certain about our claim. This only tells us how intimate, how personal, and how secured King David's relationship is with his Shepherd. I don't think he would call God as his Shepherd if he does not feel His presence in his life in a personal way. He knows firsthand how a shepherd is very much involved with his sheep, and this is how he viewed the presence of God in his life. The following statement, *"I shall not want,"* makes perfect sense as it further emphasizes the role of the Good Shepherd in King David's life. First of all, make no mistake in interpreting the first verse of the Twenty-Third Psalm. It does not mean that King David does not want his Shepherd. He does not mean *"the Lord is my Shepherd and I don't want Him in my life at all."* That's not what it means. The word *want* is synonymous with lack or neediness, and King David confirmed his confidence in his Shepherd by saying, "I shall not want." He is certain that God is someone who provides! God is someone who supplies our needs and sometimes even our wants! His provision goes in such a way that we shall no longer want for anything more. The NIV Bible used the phrase, *"I lack nothing."* It doesn't mean we will no longer lack or want anything anymore. Every person has more wants than what he really needs. The Apostle Paul tells us in Philippians 4:19, *"And my God will meet all your needs according to the riches of his glory in Christ Jesus."* This means that the Good Shepherd will take care of our needs, first and foremost. Then He will either provide us the things that we want or set our attitudes right that we shall not feel that we want anything more. He gives us that feeling of contentment or that feeling of already having enough. It has something to do with our confidence on the Good Shepherd that He will give us the right attitude and mindset of being satisfied with what we have rather than the attitude of always wanting for more. The opening verses of the Twenty-Third Psalm remind me of the prayer that the Lord Jesus Christ taught His disciples when they asked Him to teach them how to pray. Jesus said in Matthew 6:9–13, *"This, then, is how you should pray: 'Our Father in heaven, hallowed be your name, your kingdom come, your will be done, on earth as it is in heaven. Give us today our daily bread. And forgive us our debts, as we also have forgiven our debtors. And lead us not into temptation, but deliver us from the evil one.'"*

Please notice that Jesus did not say this is "what" you should pray, but instead, He said this is "how" you should pray. It is more of a guide, and it is not meant to be said repeatedly and verbatim. Prayer is communicating with God. It has to be personal and intimate and not just like some routine or vain repetition. This is a fundamental principle in prayer. When we talk to God, just remember it's like talking to our father because He is indeed our Father! Just like the

Twenty-Third Psalm, this prayer taught by Jesus Christ to His disciples starts with God, our Father, who is in heaven. I believe the reason why the *"asking for bread"* comes much later in this prayer is that Jesus wants our prayers to focus on God, first on His holiness and His glorious position or throne in His heavenly dwelling, which is well deserving and worthy of our praise and adoration. If we focus on our needs and problems right at the very start of our prayer, like asking for bread, we may fall into the trap of just focusing on ourselves, prioritizing our needs and dwelling on our problems more than giving glory to God our Father. If we prioritize these things, we miss the opportunity to praise and thank God and acknowledge His glory. This same principle is found in Matthew 6:33 where Jesus tells us to *"seek first his kingdom and his righteousness, and all these things will be given to you as well."* It's amazing that while there was no New Testament Scriptures during the time of King David, he already seriously considered those principles in the opening verse of his Twenty-Third Psalm. The first thing he did was to acknowledge that the Lord is his Shepherd, a personal Shepherd who is constantly involved in his life in a meaningful, personal, and relevant way. The same principle was followed by King David's son who was also his successor as king of Israel. King Solomon, when given by the Lord the opportunity to ask God for anything. We can find this in 2 Chronicles 1:7–12,

> If we focus on our needs and problems right at the very start of our prayer, like asking for bread, we may fall into the trap of just focusing on ourselves, prioritizing our needs and dwelling on our problems more than giving glory to God our Father.

> That night God appeared to Solomon and said to him, *"Ask for whatever you want me to give you."*
>
> Solomon answered God, *"You have shown great kindness to David my father and have made me king in his place. Now, Lord God, let your promise to my father David be confirmed, for you have made me king over a people who are as numer-*

ous as the dust of the earth. Give me wisdom and knowledge, that I may lead this people, for who is able to govern this great people of yours?" God said to Solomon, "Since this is your heart's desire and you have not asked for wealth, possessions or honor, nor for the death of your enemies, and since you have not asked for a long life but for wisdom and knowledge to govern my people over whom I have made you king, therefore wisdom and knowledge will be given you. And I will also give you wealth, possessions and honor, such as no king who was before you ever had and none after you will have."

King Solomon asks for wisdom because he wanted to bring glory to God by ruling His people with fairness and justice. He did not ask for anything that only himself will benefit from. So not only that God blessed King Solomon with wisdom, He even blessed him with the other things that he did not ask for—wealth, possession, and honor. This tells us that if we set our hearts right, if we prioritize God and seek His righteousness among others, He will take care of us. He will bless us in ways that we cannot even imagine or expect. Technically, we don't even have to ask God for anything. He knows everything and that includes our needs and also our wants. But like a father to His children, God wants us to call unto Him. He wants us to learn how to depend on Him, and in doing so, we glorify His name.

Judging from our earlier explanation on the role of a shepherd in the life of his sheep, King David definitely shall not lack anything or want something because the Good Shepherd will provide him with anything he may ever need. It tells us how big the faith of King David was toward his Good Shepherd. We need to have that kind of faith that rests on the Good Shepherd alone and does not depend or rely on someone or something else. What a great relief to know that we have Someone

> God will certainly use painful experiences so that we can be effective ministers to others who encounters a similar predicament.

who takes care of us in terms of what we need in life! One important perspective here is that if we acknowledge that the Good Shepherd knows our needs and because of our relationship with Him, we shall lack nothing. We should trust Him more than anything else.

In other times, the Good Shepherd will allow us to experience something painful or difficult for us to develop our character. This painful or difficult experience can be problems, trials, persecutions, and sufferings. We need these experiences in life in order to learn our lessons and do better next time we encounter a similar situation. Painful experiences will help us make better decisions in life and, most importantly, to be able to also minister to others. God will undoubtedly use these painful experiences so that we can be effective ministers to others who encounter a similar predicament. It will be easier for us to relate to the problems of other people and give them sound and credible advice if we ourselves have experienced similar problems first hand. This is one of the reasons why the Lord Jesus Christ, our Good Shepherd, knows our needs and our situations. He Himself has experienced all kinds of sorrows while He was here on Earth. He experienced how to be hungry, how to be denied, how to be mocked and treated unjustly. Our Good Shepherd understands our situation. He knows it. He feels it. He's been through it.

One of the most mind-boggling stories of faith in the Lord is found in the Old Testament, the book of Genesis, chapter 22 where God tested and wanted to see the demonstration of Abraham's faith by instructing him to sacrifice his beloved son Isaac. How can God ask this "hideous" thing from Abraham? Abraham knew his God. He is not that kind of God who will expect His devoted followers to sacrifice their own children blindly. There were a lot of pagan nations worshiping pagan gods during Abraham's time. Those other gods require child sacrifices but not the God of Abraham! This thought probably almost drove Abraham crazy. Isn't Isaac the son of promise through whom God shall fulfill His covenant to Abraham and his people? God's testing of Abraham defies all kinds of logic, and from our own understanding, it does not make any sense at all. How can a loving God, who has promised through a covenant that Abraham shall be a father to many nations, require that he sacrifices his beloved son Isaac? It does not make sense! Well, if Abraham does not know his God intimately, if he does not trust Him well enough, the command to sacrifice Isaac for sure does not make sense to him as well. And remember this: God is also not obliged to make sense to us. God created everything, so He owns anything and anyone here on Earth. If He demands the life from anybody, He has the full right to do so because He created each one of us and gave us life. We belong to Him. But still, it is very hard to imagine that He would command such a thing. The Bible did not tell us that Abraham hesitated at all. He was even up very early the next day. In fact, there was a clear sense of optimism in him when he told his servants that he will be back, along with Isaac, after they worship the Lord in Mount Moriah. There are two interpretations of this incident, first; Abraham could have been telling these things to his servants so they won't get in his way when he sacrifices Isaac. Second, his trust in God was so high that he believes that either God changes His mind about the command or He sends a replacement sacrifice, or even if Isaac indeed die from it, God can easily bring him back to life. In the end, we learned that God Himself provided a way out for Abraham by having a ram caught in a thicket to take the place of Isaac. This is clearly a foreshadowing of things to come. Isaac is a "type" of Christ, and one day the ultimate sacrifice of God's only begotten Son will take place in the hills of Calvary. A lot of Bible scholars believe that Calvary is at the same spot as Mt. Moriah. The big difference this time was that Christ will not be replaced by a ram or anyone else. Christ's crucifixion and death pushed through! In fact, Christ was substituting for each one of us. We should be on that cross. The death of Christ on the cross certainly did not make sense at all to His followers at that time, and it does not make sense to most of us even up to now. Some people even during our time today cannot make any sense out of the sacrifice of Christ, and I am not surprised at all. The Apostle Paul wrote in 1 Corinthians 1:18, *"For the message of the cross is foolishness to those who are perishing, to us who are being*

> **The death of Christ on the cross certainly did not make sense at all to His followers at that time, and it does not make sense to most of us even up to now.**

saved it is the power of God." But God is not obliged to justify His actions to us nor is He expected to "make sense" in our limited minds. He is God. In those times, when God does not seem to make sense in us, all we need to do is trust Him. We should trust Him that He knows what He's doing. The Creator of the Universe is not obliged to disclose all His plans to us. If He does so, it will blow our minds and will definitely not make much sense in our limited understanding.

Genesis 22:14 tells us, *"So Abraham called that place The* LORD *Will Provide. And to this day it is said, "On the mountain of the LORD it will be provided."* Jehovah Jireh means "the Lord will provide," and the Lord did, in fact provide, as in the case of Abraham. Instead of ending up sacrificing Isaac, God Himself provided a substitute, a ram caught in the thicket. As I have stressed earlier, this story is also a foretaste of a very important provision from the Lord as well. God did provide a sacrifice to atone for our sins. His name is Jesus! Truly, our Good Shepherd is our Jehovah Jireh!

David's concept of his Good Shepherd is someone who will provide for him to the extent that he will not want for any other thing anymore. He knows how a regular shepherd provides for his sheep. He knows how a good shepherd will go out of his way to find food for his flock and search for quiet waters so they can drink. He was a shepherd himself who is a good provider. He knows the drill. He is a subject-matter expert. A good shepherd provides everything the sheep needs.

As we live our lives here on Earth, we tend to aim for a lot of things or set up certain goals that we want to accomplish in life. If you are a parent like me, you want the best for your children. This is our nature as parents. We want to give them the best education possible in the best schools. We buy them clothes, we buy them toys, and we provide for their each and every need. As a father, it pains me a lot sometimes to see if my children are not able to enjoy what other kids experience—a nice vacation during summertime, latest gadgets, summer courses, extracurricular activities, shopping for nice clothes, and other things. Jesus said He came to this world for us to have an abundant life. However, I don't think He is merely referring to material abundance or material prosperity. I know that our Lord has also blessed a lot of people materially. That is a fact. We have seen devoted followers of God who are also materially prosperous, and we have also seen even people who do not believe in God seems to be doing well materially in this world we live in. Matthew 5:45 says, *"He causes his sun to rise on the evil and the good, and sends rain on the righteous and the unrighteous."* But we also know from the Bible that His closest disciples died not only with terrible and horrific deaths, but they also died in extreme poverty. They have been severely persecuted, and even those who came after them experienced terrible hardships. I would assume that Luke the physician and Paul the great evangelist had better lives (financially at least) prior to their conversion to Christianity.

One of the stories that amaze me in the New Testament is Matthew 19:16–22 where a rich young ruler approached Jesus Christ and asked Him about eternal life. Based on this story, not only that this young man was rich, he was probably beaming with pride because he thought it was enough that he had kept the commandments. But when Jesus told him to sell his possessions, give to the poor, and follow Him, the man was disappointed; and much to his chagrin, he went away sad. He simply can't just let go of his wealth. True disciples of Christ do not mind what will happen to them here on earth as they follow Christ. They know that they can be poor throughout their lives here on earth because Jesus never promises that we can all be materially prosperous here anyway. The true disciples can see beyond what is going on here on earth as they look forward to the eternal life in heaven promised to them by their Good Shepherd.

The lives of our Christian forefathers were marred by injustice, torture, and persecutions. If they suffered all their lives here on Earth, where is that abundance that Christ was talking about and was preached to others even by these same disciples? The abundance that Christ speaks pertains to spiritual abundance. It relates to a kind of contentment that is not temporary but eternal and can only be found in Christ. We can never be satisfied with the material pleasures of this world. Even the latest gadgets or the fanciest toys cannot satisfy our longing for contentment. For generations, finding worldly contentment has always been the goal of many, and this has led to major disasters, injustice, and even war. Jesus said, *"Apart from Me you can do nothing."* The true abundance coming from the Good Shepherd doesn't mean we will not want anything, but it means that He will not leave us wanting. Jesus said to the Apostle Paul, *"My grace is sufficient for you, for my power is made perfect in weakness"* (2 Cor. 12:9). I believe this is where our contentment should be based upon. Because of the grace of God through the sacrifice of Jesus, we should always feel sufficient already. If we are certain that the eternal life offered by Christ covers everything already, then contentment will soon follow.

God has made the ultimate provision for all those who will believe Him, and this is the person of His Only Begotten Son, Jesus Christ. He did not only provide His presence or His principles, He did not only perform His miracles or His healings, but also God offered no less than the life of His Only Begotten Son. God's ultimate provision is not food nor material wealth. It is something that will last certainly beyond this lifetime. Jesus died on the cross in order to provide life for each one of us, for eternity! This is the ultimate abundance that we can ever think of. It's permanent; it's not subject to decay or rust. It cannot be stolen, and most of all, it lasts for eternity.

My wife and I are blessed by the Lord with two wonderful children. Aside from our relationship with the Lord and our relationship with each other, our children are God's greatest gift for us. Not only that they are very loving and respectful, but they are also very hardworking, and they did very well in their schools. When I became a pastor, my wife and I decided at one point that she will stop working to become a full-time mother to my children and a full-time wife to me, to fully support the family and also to help me as her husband and as a church pastor. We knew that it will be a big sacrifice on her part, and we did lose quite a lot in terms of household income, and we dread the day when the time comes for our children especially our eldest to start studying in college or university. When we were in the Philippines, our daughter used to have a university educational plan, but we had to convert it to cash when we moved to Canada from the Philippines and used it to start our new life. We did not save anything for her nor did we have savings of our own. The day we feared finally came. I remember when my daughter was about to finish high school, probably in Grade 11, she asked me a question, "Dad, what's your plan for me after high school?" She wanted to go straight to university. She has no other plans but to study in one of British Columbia's major university. Being an A student since grade one, she knew she would qualify academically to any school of her choice, and she was confident she can keep up with the rigorous demands of being in a university. I was thinking of something else. I thought it would be better if she starts in a community college first and then transfers to a university in her third or fourth year. Not because I didn't believe that she can handle the pressure, but I was thinking of saving some money because it will be a lot cheaper to start in a community college first. It will also give her time to adjust coming straight from high school. Of course, I did not tell her about my plans, but my wife and I were already thinking about it. When I told her our Plan A for her to start in a community college, she wasn't very happy about it. She said if she can qualify or if she gets admitted straight to a university, why does she have to go through a community college? I saw how frustrated she was so, I told her what our Plan B was. She can go straight to university, but she has to apply for a student loan, and we are going to pay for it in the future. That was our plan— me and my wife—and we all agreed. She was happy, and we were settled, sounds like a good plan! However, I never imagined that God has something else in His divine and perfect mind. He has blessed my daughter with a lot of academic achievements graduating in high school. She was endorsed by her guidance counselor, homeroom teacher, and school principal to each and every scholarship opportunity available and applicable for her, one of which was a major scholarship from a leading university in British Columbia. Aside from her academic track record in high school, she needed to write an essay, and that essay will play a major part for her to be selected and receive the university's full scholarship award. She has written a lot of essays, and I could say that writing is one of her strengths. She does not normally consult me when she writes her essays, but in this particular case, she did, and I only suggested to add some Bible verses. Without much hesitation, she followed my advice, so she added 1 Corinthians 13:11, which says, *"When I was a child, I talked like a child, I thought like a child, I reasoned like a child. When I became a man, I put the ways of childhood behind me,"* and the other one was Matthew 6:34, *"Therefore do not worry about tomorrow, for tomorrow will worry about itself. Each day has enough trouble of its own."* We were reluctant because we did not want the school authorities at first to think that we are trying to inject something "religious" in her essay, and somehow we wanted to be politically correct. In the end, I told my daughter that God's word is powerful; it is alive and active, and this can be a good testimony for whoever will read her work. Whether she gets that scholarship or not, what is important is that God's word has been shared. I remember receiving a letter in the mail from the university stating that my daughter got accepted to the university with a five-thousand-dollar scholarship. We were so happy already at that time, but we did not realize that God wasn't finished yet. That first scholarship was only for her academic qualifications. A few weeks later, we got another letter saying that the university is taking back the initial five-thousand-dollar scholarship because she was selected for the full scholarship award! It was a tremendous blessing for our family, and my daughter got the full scholarship. It's a living testimony that we have a God who is all-powerful, and truly, He is our Jehovah Jireh! He provides! We never paid a single penny for her university expenses. We bring all glory to God because He proved not only to my daughter but also to our whole family that we have a Good Shepherd who will not leave us wanting. We should not worry about tomorrow and let God "worry" about our worries! If we fully recognize the role of our Shepherd in our lives, truly we will lack nothing. He provides us in ways and means that is beyond our comprehension. My wife has guided our children well –attending to their needs every day so they can concentrate on their studies. My wife and I recognize that even if she, for example, worked for several years, she cannot save enough money to pay for our daughter's university education. We have a Jehovah Jireh who is our Good Shepherd. With Him, we shall lack nothing.

As far as our youngest child is concerned, aside from his academic achievements, God has blessed him with a gift of music. At a young age, my wife and I can tell that he has that gift. All day long, he keeps on singing, whistling and listening to music from the Internet. Years before he studied music in his elementary school, I found a nice old flute (made in France) in our parking lot. We live in an apartment building where there is a common basement parking area. There is a portion in this basement parking near the elevator lobby entrance where any resident can leave any stuff like electronics or musical instruments or even clothes or furniture, for as long as they are in decent and working conditions, to be taken away by other residents for free. This is where I found this very nice flute. I kept it with me for more than two years, and more than once that I was tempted to sell it, but it was good that I didn't. I was never satisfied with the offers that I received when I tried posting it online. I knew that the flute is expensive, and it is a very good quality flute although it's already old. When my son needed a musical instrument in his music subject, I convinced him to choose the flute as his instrument as I remember I still have this flute being kept in the stockroom. So I brought it to a music store and had it tuned up and replaced the mouthpiece. The store clerk confirmed to me that it was indeed an expensive and good-quality flute. Since then, my son had been playing flute for his music class, and he also joined seasonal music concerts. While other kids were renting musical equipment like saxophone or clarinet or violin, my son had his own flute! We didn't even have to rent; it was his own flute! God truly provides! He didn't even want us to rent or buy; God gave my son this flute. He did not necessarily provide us with money to buy or rent a musical instrument for our son, but He provided the flute to us in a way that we can never expect. I just found it there in the parking basement. Sometimes, God's answer to our prayers is only within our reach. We just have to be aware of our surroundings and pay attention to what's going on around us. Aside from regularly playing in his school, my son is now part of the church's praise and worship team. He plays the flute almost every Sunday. Now he is able to use his gift to serve God in the ministry, and a lot of people in the church are blessed with his passion for music.

Another wonderful provision that God has blessed us with was my son's gift in playing the piano. He loves to play the piano, but he never formally took any piano lesson. We wanted to send him to summer classes, but it was costly, and we did not have any extra budget for those kinds of classes. Likewise, he also wanted to enjoy his summer vacations by playing and doing other things. One day, a goodhearted family friend in our church upgraded their son's piano and gave the older piano to my son, for free! My son's old piano did not have all the octaves, but this one was complete. He continued to listen to tutorials on the Internet and followed them using the piano that he received from our friend, so we can hear him memorizing and playing lots of songs. Every day, he played the piano, and every day, his skills were getting better and better. With no formal lessons, he learned and taught himself with the aid of the Internet. One day, my daughter challenged him to learn one of her favorite songs. So he kept practicing day after day until one day we realized that he can play the song really well. Without our knowledge, he asked his music teacher in school if he can play solo in the upcoming spring concert, and his teacher agreed. So for the first time, my son was able to perform solo in the concert in front of hundreds of people. Most soloists are the ones who are really excelling in their instruments, normally those who had formal education. After my son played the piano piece, everyone loved his performance, and he got the accolades from his classmates and teachers. The point I am driving at here talking about provisions from Lord is that we may never have resources to send him to piano school, but still, God made it happen to have him play in the concert. A lot of kids with formal music education cannot just render a solo, but here is my son who only learned how to play on the Internet using a piano given by our friend, and he was able to play solo in one of his school's major music concert. God truly provides!

We must acknowledge that if our life is fully surrendered to the Good Shepherd, there is nothing that we need that He cannot provide. A lot of times we get tempted by the enemy to look at others and feel bad about ourselves for not having the things that others have. We ask God why we cannot buy or acquire what others can. We look outside our windows and see what our neighbors have that we don't, and we feel bad. Why can't we go on an expensive vacation just like our friends? Or why can't we have a bigger house or a nicer car or a better job? When the psalmist says, "I lack nothing," he does not mean we shall have everything. That was never the point of this verse. "I lack nothing" means that God is able to give us the right mindset and attitude of our heart to know that while we cannot get everything we want in life here on earth, we become fully contented with what we have and that we are truly thankful to God our provider. This right mind-set also involves us fully trusting the Lord that our life after this life is going to be much better, far beyond our imagination. Comparing what we have with others is a clear recipe for frustration and disappointment, not only in the things that we have but also in the things that we do. What we normally do not consider is when we look at others, we only see their façade. We only see what is going on the outside, and we don't have any idea what is happening on the inside. We don't really know what's going on inside their homes or inside their lives. Some people whom we think are materially wealthy are actually the ones who are drowning in debts. They buy expensive clothes, the latest gadgets, fancy cars, and even huge houses; but in reality, they live beyond their means. The more we look at other people—how skilled they are, how smart they are, or how gifted they are—the less time we have to appreciate our own skills and talents. The more we compare what we have with others, the more we become unhappy, discontented, and disappointed with ourselves and with what we have. God has given each one of us enough skills and talents to bring glory to Him and live our lives to the fullest. Are we using those skills and talents to glorify Him? Or do we just waste time grumbling or complaining about the things that we don't have? The Apostle Paul tells us in Galatians 6:4–5, "*Each one should test their own actions. Then they can take pride in themselves alone, without comparing themselves to someone else, for each one should carry their own load.*" God created each one of us in a very unique way. We are the apple of His eyes. He has "stamped" each one of us with unique qualities and very useful skills. Have you ever wondered why no two people have the same fingerprints, eye scan, or even DNA? This is a clear proof that we are unique, and even twin siblings have very noticeable differences. God knows us in a very personal way. We need to be grateful for everything that God has blessed our lives with. We need to be contented with what we have and not be dissatisfied with the things that we don't have. The Bible tells us in 1 Timothy 6:6–11,

> *But godliness with contentment is great gain. For we brought nothing into the world, and we can take nothing out of it. But if we have food and clothing, we will be content with that. Those who want to get rich fall into temptation and a trap and into many foolish and harmful desires that plunge people into ruin and destruction. For the love of money is a root of all kinds of evil. Some people, eager for money, have wandered from the faith and pierced themselves with many griefs.*

I think the Apostle Paul has captured in the above passage the crux of being contented and not wanting for anything more. Being content is also being godly. If we just recognize the fact that God owns everything, and when He gave us life and was born into this world, we didn't have anything with us. We didn't have possessions, and we didn't know what to do anything except to maybe cry and crave for milk. God has given us everything we need, and as we get older, He kept on supplying everything to us. So whatever we have, whether we feel that it's inadequate or scarce, we should change our attitude just like King David. The Apostle Paul also mentioned something very important. He said, "For the love of money is the root of all kinds of evil." Our Good Shepherd Himself said that we cannot serve both God and money. Usually, whenever we have unreasonable wants, it all boils down to money. We think that money can buy everything we want, and sometimes, when we have lots of money, we tend to think that we don't need the Good Shepherd anymore. This is because we become so distracted with everything that money can buy or things that we can do because we have money. Paul said we may fall into *"a trap and into many foolish and harmful desires that plunge people into ruin and destruction."* This is the reason why contentment is very important. If we are contented, God, through the

Holy Spirit, will be able to minister in our lives and allow us to reach our full potential. We'll be able to keep the right attitude without getting envious of with other people. We'll be able to serve God with all our heart because we don't look at what is missing from us, or we don't look at what others have, but we only look at what God has provided us or what else can He provide.

I remember going to college was not that easy for me. My father had to ask his relatives to allow me to stay in their place in the city as we were living in a far and remote town about five hours away. Unfortunately, we were never close to our relatives in the city, so it was really an awkward situation to stay with them, but I had no choice. I was determined to finish my schooling no matter what the cost. It would have been easier to stay with anybody if we have enough money, but we did not. A lot of times I had to walk going to school in order to save on transportation fares. I remember during my first year, we were required to purchase an accounting book, but since I didn't have enough, I had to buy a secondhand one. I used my last money to buy that book, but when I opened the book, every other page was blank. In those bookstores, the policy was "no return, no exchange," so I had to go to the library, borrow a similar book, and manually copy on all of the blank pages for the missing text. I remember not regretting anything at that time. I was happy being able to purchase a book, and I know I was still in a much better position than most teens at my age who were not even able to finish high school. Even if it was hard to live with my relatives, I was still very thankful that my father didn't have to pay them anything for my stay. The funny thing was that because I had to copy so much text on the blank pages of the book, whenever I had tests and examinations, it was already very easy for me to get high grades because I was already very familiar with what was written on the book. Sometimes, our disappointments are God's appointments. We feel that we are lacking something, but in reality, God was filling in something more precious and valuable. I may have lacked the pages literally, but God was actually forcing me at that point to study the book without me realizing it. Without knowing it consciously, my Good Shepherd was showing me at that time that I shall lack nothing.

Reflection Questions

1. Can you describe a situation when God has blessed you abundantly? How long ago was that?
2. If you answered yes to number one, what have you done after that? Did you share with others this experience? Do you still share it until now?
3. Do you feel that there is a need in your life right now that the Good Shepherd has not met? What is that need?

Peace and Abundance in the Lord

He makes me lie down in green pastures,
he leads me beside quiet waters.

—Psalm 23:2

The title of this book *Quiet Waters* came from this second verse of the Twenty-Third Psalm. It relates to me as someone who grew up in a small town with my childhood spent mostly in our farm and having personally experienced spending hours beside quiet waters. It brings back some vivid memories of years ago when I was young and growing up in my hometown. Reminiscing my childhood gives me a good grasp of how vital green pastures and quiet waters are for a flock of sheep or any other kind of farm animals. A good shepherd continuously searches for green pastures and quiet waters where he could bring his flock. He knows how much the flock depends on him as their shepherd. The shepherd will not stop, and he will never get tired of looking for better places to bring his flock for them to experience abundance in terms of being able to graze on green pastures, drink safely and be refreshed on quiet waters. The Middle East in biblical times, particularly Israel, has predominantly vast desert areas, and most places are drylands. There are not that many bodies of water you can find as well as green pastures where you can take the animals for grazing. Most of the time, you will see on the dry lands are desert plants or even dead animals who cannot withstand the heat of the desert and, of course, hunger. Israel is not like North America particularly Vancouver, British Columbia, where I currently reside. Here you can find evergreen trees almost everywhere, and it rains for most times of the year, so it's always wet around you, and the weather is cold virtually the whole year-round, and you can see lush greeneries and trees all over town. It is totally the opposite in the Middle East where the shepherd and his flock have to walk in really far distances to look for ample bodies of water, green pastures, and rich vegetation. They go from one place to another searching for a new grazing place where there is an abundant source of food, clean water to drink, and a good place to rest. Like what I have mentioned in earlier chapters, sheep are high-maintenance animals. They are very picky and choosy, if I may use these terms. A sheep will not drink in running water even if they are thirsty; it distracts them, and they don't feel safe about it, so they will not normally drink when the water is flowing. Sometimes they don't want to even go near fast-flowing streams. So the shepherd had to find those places and bring his flock into quiet bodies of water like lakes, rivers, and lagoons where the sheep can feel safe and have the confidence to drink. Sometimes the shepherd has to create makeshift dams to contain the flowing waters in one area, which will allow for the sheep to have their thirst quenched. It entails a lot of hard work on the part of the shepherd, and this is one of the reasons why being a shepherd was not a popular profession in those times. It is a demanding work. It's not easy to tend for the flock of sheep, and it's a big responsibility especially if you are guarding a flock of dumb, high-maintenance, and very dependent animals.

Talking about a shepherd reminds me of my calling and present role as a pastor of a church. Pastors are shepherds of God's flock, which is the church, and just like any other shepherd, it is a serious and demanding responsibility. If a shepherd gets his flock to drink and quench their thirst in quiet waters, a church pastor has to lead his congregation also to drink the spiritual water that only Jesus Christ provides. Just like a shepherd bringing his flock to a green pasture, a pastor brings people to Christ who is the Bread of Life. In John 6:35, "Jesus declared, *'I am the bread of life. Whoever comes to me will never go hungry, and whoever believes in me will never be thirsty.'*" His responsibility is to make known to the congregation that Jesus Christ offers this living water, which is the only thing that can quench our spiritual thirst. Just like a regular flock of sheep, there are also high-maintenance sheep or members in a church congregation that the pastor has to spend more time and energy with. I remember hearing from television preacher that in the church, the pastor spends more than eighty percent of his time and energy dealing with internal issues, which usually involves difficult members. He barely has any strength left to deal with external issues like to implement evangelism programs, go on mission projects, and spread the Gospel. It is unfortunate that most churches head in this direction, and in recent years, more and more churches are becoming inward focus rather than outward. Sometimes it is even more difficult to handle people who have been Christians for a very long time rather than the new ones. They call themselves mature Christians, but a lot of times, they give more headaches to their shepherds. They are the ones who always have issues and would like to dominate every home group fellowship and Bible studies with their own problems. They are more difficult to handle. They are the ones whom the pastor always have to follow-up, checks them out from time to time, and probably spends the most number of pastoral visits. I remember what I read from Pastor Rick Warren in his book *Purpose Driven Life*; he calls these people "EGRs" or extra grace required. Sometimes, God places difficult people in our midst, and this applies not just to pastors but to any follower of Christ. Without realizing it, this is God's response whenever we pray for God to make us more patient or more loving. Difficult people are God's answers to these kinds of prayers. He will bring difficult people in our midst so we can practice loving the unlovable and learn how to be patient with them. So be careful what you pray for, as you might get them.

> **He will bring difficult people in our midst so we can practice loving the unlovable and learn how to be patient with them.**

As a shepherd, the pastor also has the responsibility to explain to the church congregation how to live a life of abundance. He relays to them what his Good Shepherd wants them to know in terms of how they conduct their lives here on earth. Living in abundance does not simply mean that we have too many blessings in the palm of our hands, and we cannot contain those blessings coming from God anymore. It is not really a picture of having too many blessings that we have become so extravagant that we are not taking care of God's resources to the point of not being good stewards anymore. But it is more of being able to handle our situation and control our reaction whether we experience excess or lack. The true abundance that the Good Shepherd provides is being satisfied and being grateful for everything that we have and certainly not becoming bitter or frustrated for the things that we don't have or the things that we lack. True abundance can be achieved even if we feel we lack something or we don't have all those other material things in life. True abundance means being good and faithful stewards of what God has blessed us with.

Do you recall that sometimes we complain too much to God when things don't exactly work out the way we planned it or when we don't exactly get what we want in life? We tend to blame God whenever He does not respond according to what we ask from Him. We expect God just to jump in and go along well with our plans. God is not a genie in a bottle where you just rub His side, and He will give you three wishes. It doesn't work that way. He is also not a vending machine wherein you just drop coins and you can pick and select what you want to receive and it will be rolling out for you in the dispenser. Sometimes we pray for a nice house over and over again; we even tell God what specific kind of house we want and the exact location where we want it. At first, we become excited and happy with any kind of house that God will bless us for as long as we own it, and we are not paying rent anymore. Initially, we would be satisfied with a small two-bedroom condominium unit or a suite in a modest apartment building. At first, we are pleased because God finally answers our prayers and blessed us with our very own house. But it will just be a matter of time before we start complaining again because we want something more, something better, and something bigger. We want an upgrade. We can always find something to complain about. It will just be a matter of time before we start to feel discontented again to the point that we begin to feel sorry for ourselves. We cry to God, and we say our house is not big enough, it's not new enough, it's not fancy enough, it's not located in a good area near a bus station, etc. We get so much pressure because our friends and neighbors start to sell their old apartment units and buy standalone or single-detached houses. Please don't get me wrong. It's not bad to dream for something big, especially for a house. What I am trying to say is that sometimes, we forced ourselves to work too much to get the things that we want in life, like a huge house. We forced ourselves to work harder and harder with two or three jobs, and we end up buying a bigger house even at the expense of our quality time with our family. I have seen couples who barely see each other anymore because they both have two or three jobs. They need to work double time because their mortgage payment is too high. They have different cars, but nobody can even drive their kids to school or church activities. Oftentimes, people who abuse themselves with too much work end up getting stressed and physically weaker, and at one point, they'll get sick. This is the time they realize what the more important things in life are. This is the time they will regret abusing themselves to death with working two or three jobs. Remember that the more important things in life are not something you can buy with money and not something that you can get by having two or three jobs. It is not about who has the biggest house or who has the fanciest cars or the most successful careers. A lot of times, when we see a dying person, when asked about what or who he wants to be with him during his last remaining hours on earth, more often than not, this person will ask for his family. Relationships suddenly matter to a person who only has a very short moment to live. It is pathetic that in the end, this dying person will desire to be with his family whom he may have rejected for a long time. It is sad that oftentimes, his children no longer have that connection with the dying person because of the years he wasted prioritizing other things more than his own invaluable time with his family.

Sometimes we even complain to God about our selves—the way we look, the way we speak, or even the way we sing. We start to ask God why we are not good looking enough, why we are not tall enough, why we are not smart enough, or why our voice is not good enough. We also complain about our families, why are we not born into a well-off family or to a smart family or a happy family. And it gets worse when we start comparing ourselves with our next-door neighbor. All we do is look out the window toward our neighbor full of envy and jealousy. We ask God, "Why are they able to buy certain things and we're not? Why are they able to go on vacation and we're not?" We're never satisfied with who we are or with what we have or with what we accomplished in life. All our lives we try and search for certain things that we thought will satisfy us and quench our deepest longings, and these are mostly material things. We dream of a big house, a fancy car, nice career, high education, authority, popularity, but little did we know it can never be enough because the things that can really and truly satisfy us are not things! We are trying to pursue the wrong desires in life, but these desires can never satisfy our longing for a more meaningful life. It's funny because oftentimes in life, we do not know what we really want. We pretend or think we know, but we actually don't. We do not really know what is best for us. The Good Shepherd, on the other hand, knows what we need and what is good for us because He knows us very well. He knows what He should give us, when He should give it, and where He should bring us. The Good Shepherd has been watching us closely, and He knows us intimately and more than we know ourselves. God never stops looking after us. He does not slumber nor sleep. In fact, the Bible tells us in Luke 2:17 that *"indeed, the very hairs of your head are all numbered."* Imagine, God knows how many hairs are in our heads! It may sound like hyperbole for some people, but I believe God knows us this intimately. He knows everything about us. Psalm 139:1–3 tells us, *"You have searched me, Lord, and you know me. You know when I sit and when I rise; you perceive my thoughts from afar. You discern my going out and my lying down; you are familiar with all my ways."* Even if we want to hide from God, we cannot do so because every place that can think of going, God knows. Verse 7 of this psalm says, *"Where can I go from your Spirit? Where can I flee from your presence?"*

Most inventors who created a certain machine would spend countless hours trying to plan, design, build and test that machine. He would be very familiar with each and every part of that machine, every nut and bolt, and every minute detail of it. If the creator happens to attend an exhibit and leave this machine in one spot, the people walking around and who will see the machine will have absolutely have no idea how this strange-looking machine operates unless they see a brochure and ask the creator. The creator knows, first and foremost, the purpose for which the machine was built for. He knows the characteristics of the machine; he knows what the machine is able and not able to do. He can tell those inquiring how to take care of the machine when to put grease on or when to do a tune-up. He knows how to optimize the machine's capacity because he created it. He also knows what can harm the machine or what can prevent the machine from performing at its highest potential. Likewise, he knows what the machine can produce and how it will benefit others.

If you want to know what is the purpose and meaning of your life, do not look at yourself in the mirror and spend countless hours trying to figure it out. Do not open the television and listen to just any person who calls himself "subject-matter expert." Do not look at your neighbor and try to pattern your life with theirs or imitate them. Ask God, the Creator Himself, about how you should live your life. He certainly knows why He created you in the first place. He is the only One who can tell you the true meaning of life and why He breathes that same life into you. There is absolutely no one else who knows us the way our Creator does.

> Knowing how much the Good Shepherd knows us intimately allows us to have that confidence in Him, and all we need to do is to trust Him.

Knowing how much the Good Shepherd knows us intimately allows us to have that confidence in Him, and all we need to do is to trust Him. His desires is to bring us to green pastures beside quiet waters, which represents abundance and peace that only He can provide. Just like what He did to the Israelites during the Old Testament times, He rescued them from slavery in Egypt and brought them to the promised land, a land flowing with milk and honey. The water that He provides will give us spiritual nourishment for eternity, and since our Good Shepherd is the Bread of Life, He helps us not only with our physical hunger, but most importantly, He satisfies our spiritual craving. If we are tired and hungry, if we are struggling in our lives, and we feel exhausted, the Lord will give us rest. Jesus said,

"Come to me, all you who are weary and burdened, and I will give you rest. Take my yoke upon you and learn from me, for I am gentle and humble in heart, and you will find rest for your souls. For my yoke is easy and my burden is light" (Matt. 11:28–30). One of the problems why a lot of people are not able to experience rest and peace in the Lord is because of pride. Even if we are already weary and burdened, sometimes we still don't want to admit it, and we don't want to surrender everything to the Good Shepherd. We are not humble enough to acknowledge that we are already failing in many aspects of our lives. All that God expects from us is the humility to admit that we failed in some areas of our lives or we are so stressed, and we need a Savior. Our yoke and burden become much lighter when we come to the Lord, and it is because He will help us carry it, and He will help us go through with it. He will not let us face our problems alone. He will always make a way to turn our burdens into blessings.

Peace and abundance is the desire of the Good Shepherd for His flock. When we hear the word *peace*, we immediately think about the absence of its opposite, like noise or even conflicts, problems, suffering, or hardships. We think about problems as the opposite of peace, and when there are no problems, we believe that is peace. We also think about conflicts as the opposite of peace. When there are no conflicts, we believe there is peace. But the reality is, there will always be problems, conflicts, hardships, or even wars. If true peace is solely dependent on what is going on around us, then I won't be surprised if very few people experience peace.

When I was a younger, my concept of peace was to go to a very quiet place without much noise from the surrounding environment. I remember when I was growing up, my father had purchased a mango farm in the Philippines. He has worked on this farm day in, day out. The farm was very close to our home, and it only takes about thirty minutes to go there on foot. The farm was on the other side of the river, so we had to cross a bridge to go there. During summertime, my older brother and I would typically go with my father early in the morning to help him out in whatever small way we can on our farm. I only did the minor tasks while the more difficult ones go to my father and my older brother. One summer, my father built a hut made of grass and "nipa," which is a common material used for building farm huts in the Philippines. The poles and floors were made of bamboo. He built it by himself, with bare hands, using only very crude tools like his jungle bolo and some carpentry tools like hammer, saw, and other stuff. My brother and I helped him a little bit, but most of the time, we were just playing while he was working on the hut. It took him probably two weeks in summer to finish it. The nipa hut only had one room, ie. living and bedroom together, which is good for about four people and the patio or terrace also serves as the kitchen at the same time. It was a nice hut. It became like our rest house which serves as our playhouse at the same time. I had a lot of fun memories inside that nipa hut. When I was in high school, every time I had a school examination like midterms or finals, I would go to that place so I can study without any distraction, and everything was peaceful and quiet. The place had no electricity, and we only used gas lamps to light the place and a small gas stove for cooking our food. At night, the only sound you can hear is the hooting of the night owls, the chirping of crickets and rustling branches of mango trees tossed by the wind especially when there's drizzling rain that made the weather really cold and wet. You can also hear the sound of waters flowing from the river bend located about five minutes away from the farm if you walk on foot. Our nipa hut at night was like a relaxing spa location that we see and experience in our time today. At that time, that was my perfect definition of peace. This place was my perfect hiding place when I was young. It was very peaceful! I was never afraid going there and sleeping overnight even if I was alone in that hut. During hot summer days, my brother and I would swim in the river nearby. I've had lots of fond memories with my family on this farm.

The farm was unfortunately sold by my father when my siblings and I were in college to support our education. All that is left with me now are blissful memories of my childhood in our farm inside our nipa hut, climbing on trees and swimming in the river. Whenever I read the Twenty-Third Psalm and read about the "quiet waters" and the "greener pastures," I cannot help but think and remember our mango farm. This place not only represents calmness, and it does not only remind me of peace, but it also represents abundance. I remember whenever it was time to harvest the mangoes, our whole family was so happy and excited. We usually would harvest baskets of mangoes from the fifty-three trees, and we would sell these mangoes to buyers and even set up a stall in the marketplace. We definitely had more than what we need! We ate a lot of mangoes during harvest season—green mango, ripe mango, mango jelly, dried mango, and all kinds of dishes that you can ever think of. My parents would even give away lots of mangoes to our neighbors. Our mango farm aptly represents peace and abundance during my younger years.

As I get older, I realize and understand that the true meaning of peace is not necessarily the absence of war or the absence of problems or the lack of conflicts. True peace is not necessarily achieved by going to a relatively peaceful place like our old mango farm or sitting beside a lake with waters so still. True peace is actually the opposite of all these. True peace is something that emanates from an inner joy, and it resonates in our whole being.

True peace is something that emanates from an inner joy, and it resonates in our whole being.

It echoes from a heart that is totally and fully surrendered to God who is our Good Shepherd. True peace is the kind of peace that comes from God alone. Jesus said in John 14:27, *"Peace I leave with you; my peace I give you. I do not give to you as the world gives. Do not let your hearts be troubled and do not be afraid."* True peace is having an inner peace of mind and emotion fully submitted to the Holy Spirit regardless of what is going on in the outside world or in our environment. A person can be in the midst of a war or in the middle of a crisis or problem and yet achieve true peace. The Bible tells us in Philippians 4:6–7, *"Do not be anxious about anything, but in every situation, by prayer and petition, with thanksgiving, present your requests to God. And the peace of God, which transcends all understanding, will guard your hearts and your minds in Christ Jesus."* The key to achieving true peace and experiencing the peace of God, which transcends all understanding is basically the following: *by not being anxious and fully trusting God in every situation and by constantly communicating to God through prayer.* It's funny because, since time immemorial, man has been in pursuit of world peace. We have seen hundreds or even thousands of advocates and initiatives promoting strategies or plans to implement global peace. Even beauty pageants, the most popular answer from the contestants is to promote world peace, and sometimes we make fun of it because we know it is easier said than done. It is ironic that even the United Nations have their "peacekeeping" forces, which are represented by soldiers with guns. It is ironic because the same weapon being used primarily in wars are carried by what they call "peacekeepers" to maintain peace. That's quite an oxymoron. I remember in the Philippines in the early '70s, the government has had several peace talks with the Communist Party, and until now, they have never reached any permanent agreement on how to settle the conflicts. Each side had always presented unreasonable demands, and they never got into any real peace treaty. Sometimes, they came up with ceasefires, but everything is temporary. Even some religions claim that they are religions of peace, but sadly, their extremists are the ones who instigate terrorist attacks, mass shootings, and social hysteria. Some individuals cannot find true peace inside their hearts coming from God, so they end up causing troubles to others. How many times have we seen in the news about senseless school shootings? It is very alarming because it only shows how much evil and corruption happens in the heart of some people. They are truly lost in the quagmire of their own failure to find true peace, and the influence they found in this world is certainly not helping. In my opinion, peace initiatives from different parts of the world are failing because they are looking at it from a different angle and from a wrong starting point. I believe the only way to achieve true and lasting peace is to start with the right source, the Prince of Peace, our Good Shepherd. Peace negotiators have totally removed God out of their equation. If people can just realize that the vacuum inside each heart longing for ultimate peace can only be filled up by the Source Himself, our Creator of the universe. We need God, period. He is the source of true peace. This world cannot give us true and lasting peace. In fact, the world is doing the opposite. With all the distractions that we face each day, and even at some point brought about by social media, achieving true and lasting peace is almost next to impossible if we rely solely on what this world has to offer.

The psalmist vividly illustrated the kind of peace that only the Good Shepherd can provide. He selflessly brings the sheep beside quiet waters. What a refreshing sight! What a calm and serene environment! At night when the flock is resting, the shepherd watches over. He barely sleeps, and he makes sure that his flock sleep in peace. If the shepherd hears something alarming like a wolf's howl or a lion's roar, he is prepared to defend his flock. He is determined to maintain peace with his flock. During the day, when there is conflict within the flock, the shepherd is always prepared to intervene. Our Good Shepherd does much more than that. Psalm 121:4 tells us, *"Indeed, he who watches over Israel will neither slumber nor sleep."*

There is a similarity between peace and abundance. If *peace* does not mean the absence of troubles or problems, *abundance* is not the presence or availability of all the things that we need or even those things that we only wanted. It is not the achievement of everything that we have planned in life especially with respect to wealth or material possessions. Abundance is not having the ability to acquire whatever we desire in this life, but instead, true abundance is having a heart that is contented with whatever we have because we recognize that everything comes from and has been graciously provided by the Good Shepherd. We have an abundance in spirit because our heart is contented with what we have, and we don't grudgingly ask for more. We don't look for things that we don't have and feel bad or inadequate with the things that we have. Abundance is having the confidence in ourselves and in everything that we have or possess because we acknowledge that all these things including our own selves and our own lives come from the Good Shepherd. Psalm 24:1 says *"The earth is the LORD's, and everything in it, the world, and all who live in it."* God owns everything. Abundance is having that grateful spirit and an endless attitude of gratitude to God who is the source of everything. Knowing that all these things that we possess came from Him, who knows us intimately and who knows what we need or will ever need, gives us that assurance that yes, we truly have that abundance of life. We know that whatever we have, whatever things we possess are more than enough to make our lives happy and complete. From our part, all we need to do is to make sure we do our best in living this life under the complete control and direction of the Good Shepherd. Then and only then we can feel and enjoy the abundance that Christ promised, lacking nothing but possessing everything we need to live this life pleasing to Him. Jesus said in John 10:10b (ESV), *"I have come that they may have life and that they may have it more abundantly."*

I learned from my father that we came from a really wealthy family. My great-grandfather was a Spanish lawyer-politician who became the first mayor of my hometown. He had acquired a tremendous amount of wealth in the form of rice fields and real estate properties. In just one or two generations, that wealth unfortunately disappeared. From my great-grandfather's time up to the generation of my grandfather, as well as my uncles and aunt, no one took great care of their wealth. My father was the youngest, and he did not even experience being sent to college, unlike his siblings. He ended up taking care of some of the rice fields of my great-grandfather as an administrator. I experienced a glimpse or taste of being wealthy when I was around seven years old wherein every time during harvest, I would see lots of rice bags in our home stockpiled in our living room, dining room, and garage. There were sacks of rice all over. That was my idea of abundance. During harvest, we would also give away bags of rice to our neighbors who were very poor. My parents had lots of friends at that time. People liked our family because we were very generous to them, especially my parents. One day, stemming from a petty argument, my father refused to work for his family and surrendered all the land titles to his grandmother. After my father abandoned the administration of his grandfather's rice fields, our life was never the same. Over the years, our family became more and more financially challenged. All that's left for the next generation like for my siblings and me were stories about how rich our family was and how big the ancestral home was and how everyone in our town asked a lot of favors from my great-grandfather. I managed to get some really old newspaper clippings written in Spanish issued in the 1920s that featured articles and news about our family. It was something to really look at and a nice story to tell my children. My father had lots of regrets in his life. One time he told me that maybe if he did not succumb to his pride and did not return the land titles to his grand-mother, we probably wouldn't have to work for the rest of our lives. It's really hard to fathom that possibility because I grew up struggling, especially during college days when I had to rely a lot on the help coming from my siblings, especially from my oldest sister. But I never had an ax to grind over my parents especially my father and I have loved them very much and deeply appreciated their sacrifices to give us the best life possible. They taught us wonderful lessons in life, and we have seen how much love they have given to my siblings and me. I respected them a lot, and now looking back, I knew God had a purpose why our family had to experience everything that we had experienced. Growing up in a situation where money is tight helped me to become more hardworking and thankful for whatever blessing God has provided along the way. When I fully surrendered my life to the Good Shepherd, I even understand further that God never promised that we shall always enjoy material abundance here on Earth. He may have blessed some people based on His own will and decision, but the abundance that He promises starts from our heart's contentment with the help and guidance of the Holy Spirit up to the time we fully experience the ultimate blessings of heaven. The Bible says in 1 Corinthians 2:9, *"No eye has seen, what no ear has heard, and what no human mind has conceived"— the things God has prepared for those who love him."* In short, we have no idea what God is planning for each one of us. God has revealed some of it to the Apostle John during his exile in the island of Patmos where he wrote the book of Revelation. Through him, we got a glimpse of heaven here and there, but I believe words are never invented yet as to how to describe what God's definition of true abundance in terms of what He has prepared for each one of His children in heaven. What we need to do while we are here on earth is to trust Him even more, especially during those times that we feel we are lacking some things in our lives. As our Good Shepherd, He takes care of us, and we shall lack nothing, and that is all we need to know.

When I moved to Canada as a new immigrant with my family, I was so determined to find a job. I knew that it would just be a matter of time before our pocket money will all be used up. I learned from a friend that he was working for one of the major universities in British Columbia as a cleaner. I thought if this guy can do it, and he is much older than me, then I believe I can do it as well. So I applied even for a temporary basis. My wife and I didn't tell this job to our children, and we thought they might be disappointed as well and feel bad for me. So I joined him, got interviewed, and that was my first job. I only lasted for two days because the job was very tough and physically demanding. I figured out that he was assigned to clean during the day when the students were mostly there, so there wasn't that much to clean, but I was assigned to work at the graveyard shift when there was no one else except the cleaners, and we just had to clean all night long. So the cleaner's work at night was like ten times more difficult compared to the cleaner's work during the daytime. On my first night, I got to clean fifteen washrooms and a huge cafeteria. My second night turned out to be even tougher. I was assigned to clean ten laboratory rooms, and this scared me a lot because of a lot of leftover chemicals and used syringes that needed to be disposed of, and at that time, my medical coverage has not come up yet. I was so depressed and frustrated, and I remember when I was mopping the cafeteria at midnight which was the size of probably two basketball courts, tears were flowing in my eyes, and I didn't understand why God has brought me to this strange but definitely not an exciting place. If I were not a Christian, I would probably even be scared because I was all alone in the building, and all I saw was my reflection on the glass walls of the cafeteria. At the end of my shift, I was so exhausted that I slept on the train and missed my stops for two consecutive nights. I also felt so dirty, and I had very little self-esteem. So I quit after the second day, but I will never ever forget that experience. God certainly taught me a lot in that two days, which probably I haven't learned in twenty years. After a week, the Lord has blessed me with a stable job in a bank that was more in line with my profession. Every time my wife and I would talk about my experience cleaning in that university, we would just laugh hard. It was a tough experience during that time, but as I got over it and moved on, the more I appreciate the lessons that I had learned, and no matter what kind of job that was, it was still certainly a provision coming from my Good Shepherd. During those times that I was so desperate in finding a job, He certainly gave me one when I most needed it.

I thought I would never see that university again as it brings bittersweet and also funny memories. After about five years, by the grace of God, my daughter graduated from high school with high academic honors, and she also got the full scholarship award from that same university. Our whole family was invited to visit the university for a welcome reception. I was so excited because this time, I came back to the same university as a guest of honor, and we had dinner with key university officials with no less than their university president. At that time, my daughter hasn't decided whether she would enroll in that university or not because she had other outstanding offers. This dinner was really intended to convince my daughter to enroll in this university and to give us a tour of the school. It was a very heartwarming and humbling experience for us, and I never imagined that we would be honored in that way. It was funny because when the school officials were giving my family a tour of the university, my daughter was surprised that I seem to know each and every major area in the school. She asked me why, and I just smiled. I told her, "*I've was here five years ago.*" God has His unusual way of lifting us up beyond our expectation or imagination. Imagine, the first time I was there was to clean fifteen washrooms, and then five years later, our family was having dinner with the university president! But God wasn't finished yet. Another five years passed, and our family came back again for another dinner at this same university with the president and with the chairman of the board of regents. This time because our daughter had already completed her degree and was awarded the dean's medal. We even had to sit in the front row during her convocation. God's abundance is something that we cannot fathom, and He has His own way of lifting us up beyond our wildest dreams.

If we have the right attitude of abundance, it empowers us to be generous and willing to give back to the Lord what He expects from us. He blesses us abundantly for us to bless others in return. He expects us to be willing channels of His blessings. Sometimes we thank the Lord when our blessings seem to be too overwhelming, and we cannot contain them anymore. I have seen families who have been blessed by the Lord with so much material blessings that they can buy the biggest house; they can go on expensive vacations two or three times a year; and they have all the expensive gadgets, the fanciest cars, and the best education for their children. Not only that, they can afford to get expensive insurance coverages, pension plans, huge savings in their bank accounts, and a lot more. I heard from my good friend in the church that there are three kinds of people when it comes to generosity in this world—those who are generous to themselves but not to others, those who are generous to others but not to themselves, and those who are generous both to themselves and others. There is nothing wrong with being generous to ourselves and our immediate families. But sometimes have we ever wondered why God had given some of us a lot of blessings way and above what we truly need in our lives? Do we really think those blessings are intended just for us to consume and enjoy? I believe that God has blessed us so much sometimes because He wants us to bless others. Those "extras" are not really meant for us, but they are given to us so we can have the opportunity for others to feel the abundance from the Good Shepherd through us. If we feel that godly abundance in our hearts, we should not have any challenge or difficulty giving away some of it to others.

I praise God because writing this book has given me peace and a feeling of abundance as well. It is a blessing to be able to experience peace and abundance even during the process of completing this work as it has kept my mind away from a lot of things or even from those days I had my own share of worries in life. It allows me to express my innermost thoughts and speak my heart's desires with the calmness and assurance that God will hopefully one day allow me to share those thoughts with others. I have prayed hard for God to let me finish this book, and it is a great privilege to have this published. By the time you are reading this book, and for every other person who will do the same, God has indeed answered my prayers, and I hope and pray that you will achieve that true and lasting peace and abundance that you have been searching for in your life as well.

Reflection Questions

1. Can you describe a situation wherein you have been so deeply troubled and it seems that peace is impossible to find?
2. Have you experienced really lacking something you need like basic necessities? How did you get out of that situation?
3. Have you ever been a channel of blessing to someone? Can you recall your experience?

What Profit Is a Man?

He restores my soul;
He guides me in the paths of righteousness,
For His name's sake.

—Psalm 23:3

The psalmist tells us that Good Shepherd restores our soul. It's very important, therefore, to first understand what the soul is and how it plays a very important role in our lives. The Hebrew word used in the Old Testament for the soul is *nephesh*, which means *"the inner being of man"* or the *"seat of emotions and passions."* Similarly, the Greek word used in the New Testament for the soul is *psuche*, which means *"the soul as an essence which differs from the body and is not dissolved by death"* and *"the seat of the feelings, desires, affections, aversions.³* The Bible tells us that a man is a triune being as we are composed of a body, a soul, and a spirit. This is interesting because some people say that this composition somehow parallels the triune Godhead or the Holy Trinity. Whenever I think of this reality about the composition of man, I am always reminded of the analogy of the light bulb that interestingly has three components as well. The first component is the bulb, which represents the body. Just like the light bulb, the body of a person is like a shell as it covers everything inside. It is the visible component or the corporeal aspect of a human being. The body is what you see on the outside, and it is the one that gets older, that needs work out, and the one that returns to the ground when a person dies. The second component of the light bulb is the electricity that flows through the wires, through the fuse, and up to the filament. The electricity represents the spirit. Just like electricity, the spirit is something we cannot see, but we know it's there because it brings life. The Bible tells us in Genesis 2:7, "*Then the Lord God formed a man from the dust of the ground and breathed into his nostrils the breath of life, and the man became a living being.*" The interaction or synthesis, if I may use the term, of the electricity and the bulb produces the light. In the same manner, the interaction of the man's body and spirit forms the soul. The light represents the soul. It is the product of the spirit and body. Just like any other product, the soul can be a good soul or a bad soul. This may be a poor analogy, but I think the light bulb visually describes how God has designed a man.

I am sure you have heard many people saying that a man is a physical being or a body with a soul and spirit. But understanding what the Scripture says regarding our Creator who is a Spirit being and the assurance that when a believer dies, his body goes back to dust but his spirit lives on to be with the Lord tells me that man is actually and in reality a Spirit being with a physical body and not the other way around. This definition looks at who we really are from a different angle, and that is from God's perspective. God is spirit, so He created spirit beings being made in His likeness and image. This is the reason why Jesus told Nicodemus in the third chapter of John that we need to be "born again" in the Spirit. It wasn't easy for Nicodemus even if he was a learned man of the law to understand what Jesus meant. He even asked Jesus what it meant to be "born of the Spirit." Of course, Jesus was referring not to the flesh but to something intangible, something eternal. This is also the reason why the psalmist tells us that our Good Shepherd refreshes our soul. God is more interested in the condition of our spirit and our souls more than our body or anything else physical because He looks at it from the point of view of eternity. God knows that our spirit and soul are eternal and will outlast this body that we have and this world where we are living. Why is it important for the Good Shepherd to restore our soul? It is our soul that faces the most difficult and most challenging situations. It is our soul that grieves; it is our soul that gets depressed or gets frustrated; it is our soul that makes the decision whether we want to follow God or not. We hear people sometimes tell another person, *"That person has a good soul or that person has a bad soul.*" It is because our soul represents who we truly are—our personality, our character, our whole being. Sometimes, when the soul is troubled or stressed, it even manifests in our physical well-be-

> **It is our soul that yearns for love, for attention, and for relationships. It is our soul that longs to worship an almighty God.**

ing. We get sick, we lose appetite and lose weight whenever our soul is deeply stressed. One important aspect of our soul is its capacity to determine what is right or wrong. This is the reason why whenever we hear people praying to God, they want God to "save their souls." It is our soul that yearns for love, for attention, and for relationships. It is our soul that longs to worship an almighty God. It is very comforting to learn that our Good Shepherd refreshes and restores our soul. God knows how badly we need this refreshing and restoration especially as we go through the challenging lives we have here on earth. When our Good Shepherd restores our soul, I am reminded of a classic old vehicle like the Gran Torino, which came out in the late '60s. In order to make this car fully functional for our driving conditions today, it needs to be repaired, renovated, and brought back to its original condition. Sometimes, restoration of an old vehicle is even more expensive than to buy a brand-new car. However, classic vehicles are restored because of its sentimental value and impressive reputation. The soul is the deepest part of our being, and since we owe our lives to God, He is the only one who can restore our souls. Our soul can only be restored if we have surrendered our lives to the Good Shepherd. We cannot expect Him to restore us if we are not part of His flock in the first place. Our souls must have been first redeemed by Jesus Christ by His grace through our faith in Him. If you are a truly born again in Christ, you can for sure experience those times of refreshing that results from the restoration of our soul by the Good Shepherd.

On the night Jesus was betrayed and was praying at the Garden of Gethsemane, He prayed to God the Father, and He said in John 12:27, *"Now my soul is troubled, and what shall I say? 'Father, save me from this hour'? No, it was for this very reason I came to this hour."* At that point, Jesus was comforted by the Father. Luke 22:43 tells us,

"An angel from heaven appeared to him and strengthened him." The same is true for us, God's sheep. When our soul is troubled, our Good Shepherd is always there to restore our souls and comfort us with His angels. Unlike the Lord Jesus Christ, our soul becomes troubled sometimes because of sin. The third verse of the Twenty-Third Psalm gives us the confidence that the Good Shepherd can assuage all kinds of worry, guilt, bitterness, anger, and resentment because He knows what we exactly need in order for our soul be restored.

Aside from the Bible, the book of Pastor Rick Warren called *Purpose Driven Life* has produced the most profound influence on my Christian life. I got an early copy of this book in 2003, and by that time, it was already selling around six million copies all over the world. I am so amazed by how the Lord has blessed Pastor Rick and his book. I visited Saddleback Church a few years ago, and I had seen how God has blessed their church in terms of facilities and membership. I read the *Purpose Driven Life* book from cover to cover several times and listened to its audiobook version as read by Pastor Rick himself over and over again while driving my car. I hope and pray that this book of mine *Quiet Waters*, even in a much smaller way, will also have a significant and meaningful impact in your life and humbly used by the Lord to change your perspective about Him as your Good Shepherd. Pastor Rick wrote in his book that *"God is more interested in what we are than in what we do. We are human beings, not human doings. God is more concerned about our character than our career, because we will take our character into eternity, but not our career."*[4] God is interested in making our relationship with Him to be more intimate and to be more personal. This reminds us how the Christian life is to be lived. It all starts with our relationship with God. If we want to understand more how to get through this life, we should not look to our left or right, but instead, we should look up and look within. We rest in Christ by being still and by fully knowing that He is a loving God and that He is our Good Shepherd. With this relationship, He restores our soul and guides us in righteous paths. This is where our careful evaluation of church activities or ministry involvement comes into play. It does not mean that our activities and service are not important, but we need to carefully evaluate if we are doing it and we are getting involved for the right reasons. We need first to make sure that our relationship with Christ is in the right place and it is authentic before we get ourselves very much involved with church ministries. The Bible tells us that even before Christ started His earthly ministry, He was first baptized by John. Many Christians and many churches have this backward. Many Christians run around and get themselves so busy doing ministry work until they are too tired to continue. And only when they have no physical or emotional strength left do they stop and rest. At some point, some people do not know why they are doing the things they are doing in the first place. They miss the point that Christianity is primarily a matter of relationship, not a religion or religious activity. It all starts with God. It points back to our Creator. This relationship first evolves around God Almighty as we are expected to love Him with all our heart, mind, soul, and strength. Our relationship with God overflows into our relationship with other people. We cannot say we love God if we cannot love others; it is simply a contradiction. To be involved with too much activity without a relationship misses the entire point of living this life, and this is the common blunder that many Christians make. We run around attending church meetings, implementing programs, planning budgets, teaching the Bible, and we forget the reason why we are doing those things in the first place. Sometimes we get so immersed with church policies like implementing church discipline and pointing out the mistakes of those people who work with us in the ministry while missing out the more important virtues of love, mercy, and grace.

One time, Jesus visited a town called Bethany at the home of Martha and Mary. We can find this story in the Gospel of Luke, chapter 10. They were the sisters of Lazarus whom we will see dying later in the Gospel John chapter 11 and brought back to life by Christ. During His visit to the home of this family, Jesus gave a fundamental lesson on the problem of too much "religiosity." Martha was so excited about all the preparations she had to make because of Jesus's visit. I would imagine that this family is a close friend of Jesus, and Martha just wanted to be sure that they will be a hospitable host for him. I would think she cleaned their home very well and eventually was too busy in the kitchen. Mary, on the other hand, sat on the feet of Jesus and was listening to everything He had to say. Then at one point, Martha even complained to Jesus the way Mary was not helping her. *"Martha, Martha,' the Lord answered, 'you are worried and upset about many things, but few things are needed—or indeed only one. Mary has chosen what is better, and it will not be taken away from her'"* (Luke 10:42). Martha for sure had very good intentions. She just wanted to be a good host, but in the course of doing that, she became a bit demanding and gave her Lord a command. She wanted Jesus to instruct Mary to assist her in whatever she was doing. The Good Shepherd can see through Martha's soul, and He knew that she was worried, and she had no joy in her heart while serving. He told Martha that "few things are only needed." Jesus does not need an elaborate dinner or grandiose ceremony. He is the perfect embodiment of humility. Jesus never loses His focus. He reminded Martha that Mary's decision to sit at His feet and worship him was a better choice than what Martha has chosen. I love this example because it speaks realistically even to our time today. Too many Christians today are unfortunately focused on serving and not on the Savior. Sometimes people who are too busy in life and even in church ministry have very little time to speak with the Lord or listen to what He has to say. I am obviously referring to prayer and reading God's Word, the Bible. How many of these busy-bees have time to have an intimate moment with God, just like what Mary did? And worse, they complain about others who are not doing things their way which is a lot of times a defense mechanism and a way to justify themselves, and in their desire to become better, they become bitter. There are a lot of modern-day Marthas in our time today. They thought it's all about quantity—how many ministries they are involved with, how much money they donate to the church and to the poor, how much knowledge they have about the Bible, how many people they can convince to support their fund-raising projects, and a lot of other "how much." In reality, it's all about quality. It's spending quality time with God. Mary spent quality time with Jesus, and Jesus spent quality time with God the Father. How much time do we spend communicating to Him through prayers? How much time do we spend listening to Him through reading His word, and how much time we actually apply in our lives what we have learned from the Bible? All these other "works" or activities will flow naturally from our commitment to God. When our foundation with God is right, and our relationship with the Good Shepherd is strong, we will not experience burnouts and will have more capabilities to handle stress and most especially in dealing with frustrations in the ministry. The apostle Peter said it best when he wrote in 1 Peter 4:9–11:

> *Offer hospitality to one another without grumbling. Each of you should use whatever gift you have received to serve others, as faithful stewards of God's grace in its various forms. If anyone speaks, they should do so as one who speaks the very words of God. If anyone serves, they should do so with the strength God provides, so that in all things God may be praised through Jesus Christ. To him be the glory and the power for ever and ever.*

I remember a funny story that I heard from one of my good friends in the church. It is about a man whose job was to dig the ditch. He was once asked by a young boy, "Sir, why do you dig the ditch?" He said he digs the ditch so he can have a job. The young boy asked, "Why do you need a job?" He replied that he needed a job to earn money. The young boy continued asking, "Why do you need money?" The man replied that he needed money to buy food. The young boy asked, "Why do you need to buy food?" The man replied that he needed to buy food so he can eat and be strong. The young boy asked him one more time, "And why do you need to be strong?"

The man finally replied, "I need to be strong so I can dig the ditch!"

This may be a funny story, but it tells us the irony of life for most people. A lot of people just go through the motions of their everyday lives, and oftentimes they lose track of the reason why they are doing what they are doing in the first place. It's the vicious cycle of life, and they can easily get caught up with the humdrum of each day, and they lost touch with their primary reason for being. This is how we get so weary and stressed. This is how we get so exhausted in this life. When we keep on doing what we are doing and we just simply lost the reason why. King Solomon had something to say about this. He wrote in Ecclesiastes 2:22–23, *"What do people get for all the toil and anxious striving with which they labor under the sun? All their days their work is grief and pain; even at night their minds do not rest. This too is meaningless."* I believe this is a wake-up call for all of us. There is nothing wrong with working hard, and there is nothing wrong with wanting to provide a very good future for our family, especially for our children. I do hope that we are doing it for the right reasons. I have seen families torn apart because the parents were only focused on work, work, work. In North America, some parents don't get satisfied with one, two, or even three jobs. Their lives get better financially, but it comes at a very high cost. They end up sacrificing their quality time with their family, they can barely go to church, and most of them can't even keep a regular praying habit and reading of God's Word. A lot of people nowadays are like that man who digs on the ditch. They just go round and round in their lives with no clear directions and meaningful purpose. They only look at what is here and now. They don't look far ahead, and they don't look deep within.

The Good Shepherd gives us meaning in life. He gives us the reasons behind why we should do certain things. He is the source of our true joy in whatever things we do in this life. The Bible is very clear about our purpose here on Earth. Isaiah 43:7 tells us, *"Everyone who is called by my name, whom I created for my glory, whom I formed and made."* We are created by God to give Him glory. This is the path that each one of us should take. Companies have vision statements because it guides them and directs all their activities toward achieving that vision. Christians should always look toward glorifying God in everything that they do. For each and every activity we undertake, we should always ask the question: "Am I bringing glory to God?" If our answer is no or maybe, then we should rethink why we are doing it in the first place. Doing things for a different purpose stresses us and will not give us true joy and accomplishment. The Bible tells us in Colossians 3:23, *"Whatever you do, work at it with all your heart, as working for the Lord, not for human masters." Glorifying God is the all-encompassing, over-arching vision statement of every man.* Just like corporations, if glorifying God as stated by the Prophet Isaiah is our vision statement, the Great Commission is our mission statement since one of the ways that we can truly glorify God is by making sure that we share the Gospel of Jesus Christ to others.

Another negative impact of being activity-centered instead of being Christ-centered is the effect it has on our immediate families. In my years as a pastor, I have seen how one member of the family, like the husband or the wife, has been so involved in church ministries, but when the person gets home, there are lots of problems that the person needs to deal with. Sometimes a very active person in the ministry barely has time for his or her family. From the point of view of the person's family, there is really no difference whether the person goes to a party on a Friday night with his or her drinking buddies or attends a ministry meeting because in both instances, the person is not there for the family. He or she is not there to be a parent to the children or be a spouse. There is a great danger in all this. We cannot justify our being an absentee parent or absentee spouse just because we are doing ministry work and be not around for our family. There is an almost invisible line that divides one's sincere devotion to God's work and the pride to "show off" to people. Only God sees the heart, and it is so easy to get caught up in this problem, and I will discuss this a little later in this chapter. Even for pastors, we have heard so many news about how one really good and active preacher lost control of his family, and the result is devastating. I cannot say it is easy as I have children of my own, and I am far from over in terms of seeing them do well in life and achieve their full potentials. When the child is grown up, especially when they move out and start living on their own, they already make decisions for themselves. Parents can only do so much especially when the children still live with them. Their role is to be there for their children as much as they can and, most especially, teach their children about their reason for being, and that is to glorify God. Proverbs 22:6 tells us to *"start children off on the way they should go, and even when they are old they will not turn from it."* This verse tells us that parents can only "start off" their children and be ready to give a piece of advice on every step of the way. It is like teaching them the basics or the foundation of life. However, at certain points in their lives, our children will have to choose their own path and make their own decisions. Sometimes, no matter what their parents do, they still make the wrong decisions and commit mistakes. While this is heartbreaking for parents, sometimes our children learn the most important lessons in life through the mistakes and the wrong decisions they make. We always hear the saying, "Experience is the best teacher." God sometimes allows us to make wrong decisions and commit mistakes, and we are like our children who are stubborn and does not take heed of the advice coming from their parents or from those people who care for them. Our mistakes in life, which leads to serious problems, are sometimes God's way of calling our attention. It is like a wake-up call. Don't we pray the most when we have serious issues? Don't we call to God more often when we are sick or when our loved ones are in the hospital? If we handle these difficult situations right and according to how God wants us to handle them, we learn very important lessons in life, and probably we can even help others deal with their own problems.

Our Good Shepherd is definitely interested in refreshing our souls and in guiding us on the right paths. This section is entitled "What Profit Is a Man" because I am making reference to my own life verse in Matthew 16:26, i.e. *"What good will it be for someone to gain the whole world, yet forfeit their soul? Or what can anyone give in exchange for their soul?"* This verse was shared to me by my wife a few years ago. It was her way to constantly remind me that it is more important to please God more than anyone else in this world. I made it as my life verse from then on. It is more important to focus on things with an eternal value from an eternal perspective rather than to be concerned with temporal things from a temporal perspective. There is a tendency for us to get so attached to this world, and in the process, we try to please men without realizing that we are missing the most important thing in our life, which is our relationship with God.

I would say our souls are very important as emphasized in this verse. God wants us to understand that the purity of our souls is much more important than any other accomplishment in this life. People might honor us because of all the things that we can accomplish in this world, but if those accomplishments jeopardize the condition of our souls, God wants us to think twice. Jesus said in Matthew 10:28, *"Do not be afraid of those who kill the body but cannot kill the soul. Rather, be afraid of the One who can destroy both soul and body in hell."* I know that most people talk a lot about the things that they like or even the things their love to others. You will know if a person loves cars because he can talk to you for hours about the latest models and features of different cars. I had an officemate who was like that. He was a very quiet person, but once you bring up a topic about cars, he could go on forever. He knows the latest trends in the car industry, and he is always interested in having a good conversation about it. Some people love to talk about gadgets or music or movies. A person who speaks a lot about something is a reflection of what they love the most and what is important in their lives. If you love God, you will talk about Him more often. If you care about Him, you will obey His commands, which can be found in the Scriptures.

It is very important to have your own life verse, and I strongly suggest you pick one. Matthew 16:26, as I have mentioned earlier, is my life verse. It is a good reminder of what is important for me as a person. Having a life verse allows you to remember what God's word is for you, and there is a big chance that you will share and talk about it more and more to others. Having a life verse is some sort of a guide like a vision or a motto as to how we conduct our lives.

There was a time in my life when I was only concerned with the things of this world. I was focused on material things, on the tangibles and the visible elements in life. I was mainly concerned with my career, with earning money, and most especially with what people would say about me. I was very competitive and has worked very hard in any job that I have undertaken. Things about God or religion is probably the last in my list. I would go to church regularly, just like what I did since I was young, but I was just going through the motion, and I did it out of tradition and again, for people around me to like me and be impressed with me. As a young boy, I served in the church as an altar boy for almost eight years, and my idea of salvation then was everything about what I was doing or working "for the Lord." I thought of it as a loyalty point system similar to what we see in credit cards or membership cards nowadays. As I serve in the church during my early years as a young boy, I believe I was accumulating points good enough to secure my place in heaven. I thought when I grow up, I will be fine and no need to worry about salvation. Little did I know then that *all our righteous acts are like filthy rags* (Is. 64:6).

Years later, after finishing college in Manila and becoming a CPA, I worked as an auditor with the biggest bank in the Philippines at that time, and this was where I met one of my supervisors in our department. He was a Baptist Christian, very passionate, and his whole family was serving the Lord. His son was even going to a Bible school. He was very passionate about his faith, and I believe he can sense that there is something that God wants him to do for me. He loved to bug me, every so often during lunch breaks, holding the Four Spiritual Laws gospel tract of Campus Crusade in his hand. He would like to ask me if in case I die on that evening or on the following day if I know where I am going. I was always so offended, so furious, and so indifferent to him. Obviously I just can't be that mad because he was my supervisor, and I was thinking if I didn't get to be on good terms with him, my career would suffer. My usual response to him was, "Of course, I know where I am going," but I would blurt out that response out of anger taking offense at him, but little did I know, God has been knocking at the door of my heart as early as then and through this person. He was already planting the seed of His word for my salvation. He would always have a follow-up question, "Are you sure?"

In my mind, I was thinking, *How can you even be sure about those things?* I never appreciated my supervisor for what he did to me. To me, at that time, he was a nuisance. He would even hold Bible studies during lunch breaks with some other Christians in the department. I find it a bit annoying to see them do that. I resigned from that bank in 1995 and worked in different companies after, and I never heard anything from my supervisor. He never saw me accepting Jesus. He knew I was attending church sometimes, or I would occasionally join his office Bible study from time to time, but maybe in his mind, all his efforts had gone into waste. We did not work together long enough for him to see the fruit of his labor. It took maybe another five years before I truly surrendered my life to Jesus Christ, and this was after some problems I encountered in my marriage. Perhaps if I have listened to God's voice much earlier, my life would have been a bit different. Maybe if I have listened to my supervisor, I would have avoided a lot of wrong decisions that I made in my life. Here is the amazing thing that has happened after several years. I became a Christian in the year 2000, and after migrating to Canada in 2005, I became a pastor. In 2013, my family visited the Philippines, and there was this one time despite our very busy schedule that we went to the mall to meet some of our friends. I was standing in front of the restaurant waiting for some church friends whom we were going to have dinner with, and guess who I saw, of all people, walking inside the mall and approaching toward my direction? It was my supervisor! It was a big surprise for both of us that of all the people that I can meet at that time, I met him. I believe God gave me the opportunity to tell him that all his efforts years ago were not wasted. I am a living testimony of his persistence and perseverance in sharing the Gospel. In our short conversation, he told me how glad he is knowing how I am now serving the Lord as pastor. He also told me that he was sort of "backsliding" at that time but was very much inspired upon meeting me. He knew that God has blessed him by blessing me. I know in my heart that God will take care of him and will not let him fall away.

For the past few years that I have been involved in the ministry, I realized that there is a very thin line that demarcates pleasing God and pleasing others. I think this is one of the areas that church leaders especially pastors should carefully watch out for. It is so easy to be caught up in the temptation of pleasing men rather than glorifying God. Sometimes we get so engrossed with the accolades that we receive from people, and we forget to give the glory back to God. As a pastor, it is very easy to fall into this trap that whatever wonderful deeds we have done especially in the church are just coming from our own efforts and not from God. My wife would always remind me that every time somebody says something good about me or my work in the ministry, I should quickly give glory to God because the good words can get into my head and turn into pride. A lot of times, church members would approach me after the service and say nice words, especially about the sermon. I make it a point that I praise our God more than anything or anyone. The enemy is waiting for an opportunity to steal the reward that is appropriated for us because of these accomplishments. The enemy wants us to take selfish pride in whatever we do and miss out the real blessing by acknowledging the source of our greatness and that is our God Almighty.

When Jesus Christ was with His disciples on their way to Capernaum, His disciples were arguing who was the greatest among them. They kept quiet when Jesus asked them, but Jesus, knowing everything, called the twelve and said, *"Anyone who wants to be first must be the very last, and the servant of all"* (Mark 9:35). Then Jesus took a little child in his arms. He said to them in Mark 9:37, *"Whoever welcomes one of these little children in my name welcomes me; and whoever welcomes me does not welcome me but the one who sent me."* He was teaching them the value of humility. Children, at that time, were not really being taken seriously in the society. The people around them didn't recognize the impact of children in their lives. Therefore, Jesus used the example of children, and He wanted His disciples to treat them right, with humility and respect just like any other person whose standing in the society is not very significant.

The Twenty-Third Psalm tells us that the Good Shepherd refreshes our soul. Every time we see the word "refreshes," we automatically think of a scenario that we are so thirsty, and only a glass of cold water can refresh us. Have you ever felt being so thirsty? I remember the first time my whole family went to Disneyland in Anaheim, California. Coming from Vancouver, Canada, the temperature in California was really very warm in comparison. As we walked around the Disneyland park for hours, I was so thirsty. I have never felt that thirsty in my life. I had to drink lots of bottled water even if it was very costly because that was the only thing that can refresh me at that time. During the time of our Lord Jesus Christ, He met a Samaritan woman near the well. The unusual thing about this story was that traditionally, it was not a pleasant sight for a Jewish man to talk to a woman in public, more so a Samaritan. In the culture of those days, women did not have the same social status as men and for a Jewish man to talk to a Samaritan woman was definitely a cultural taboo. Samaritans and Jews had a long feud over generations that is why even Jesus's disciples cannot understand what was going on. They just left Jesus Christ to get some food, and when they came back, here was Jesus talking to the Samaritan woman, which was surely against the norm. Although Jesus asked for water from the woman to quench His physical thirst, He was actually there to offer this Samaritan woman living water that can refresh her soul and quench her spiritual thirst. What a great contrast! The woman thought that she was the one quenching Jesus's thirst after a long walk, but in reality, the Samaritan woman had great need, and she was thirsty. Her soul was actually thirsty, and Jesus made her aware of that situation. Jesus does not look at our race or our background or our ethnicity. He offers the same living water to anyone who is willing to receive Him. This water that Jesus offers quenches our spiritual thirst and refreshes our soul for eternity. Just like a sheep, you may have been in this long and arduous journey all your life. You may have been walking and panting or probably going round and round the same road. You are tired, thirsty, and probably does not have any more energy to move forward. You are just at a point of giving up. You need the kind of spiritual water that only Jesus can provide. By surrendering your life to Him, you get to partake of this water, just like what the Samaritan woman experienced. Jesus was gracious enough to offer the woman this water regardless of the norm of those times and regardless of her background. She went home telling everyone about her experience, and people believed her. In the Middle-Eastern world where the weather is warm and humid, refreshing water is always a pleasant experience, and water is always what the travelers are looking for. What is also interesting in this encounter was that Jesus pointed out to the woman her

When we surrender our lives to Christ, we have to come clean. We have to lift up every aspect of our lives to Him, whether good or bad.

current situation, that she was living with a man who was not her husband. Sometimes, when we are in the act of sinning, it is very hard to us to realize our situation and true condition. God usually will send someone to cross our path and point out our mistakes. The woman could have denied her situation with Christ although it will be pointless as Jesus is omniscient. He knows everything. When we surrender our lives to Christ, we have to come clean. We have to lift up every aspect of our lives to Him, whether good or bad. If we want Jesus to be our High Priest and Mediator, if we want Jesus to be our Good Shepherd, we have to open up ourselves to Him. No hold-backs, and no more pretensions. We may be able to fool each and every person that we might come across but not the Good Shepherd. Sometimes on the outside, we appear quite different and impressive. It's as if nothing is going wrong in our lives. We come to church, we serve in the ministry. Our family seems perfectly all right, but when we go home, that's where we have to confront our personal issues. A lot of times, our children see the real "us." This is the reason why they are the most severely affected whenever we have issues. The Samaritan woman came clean to Christ. She did not deny or "justify" any of the things that Jesus told her. She just had to admit that the person she was having a conversation with was no less than the Messiah. All she wanted was to partake of that living water that only Jesus Christ alone can offer.

The Good Shepherd does not only refresh our soul with His living water, but He also guides our paths. A lot of people are getting tired of their journey in life, and they feel thirsty and hungry; and a lot of times, they already want to give up. This is because they are going in the wrong direction in their life's journey. A lot of times, we go on circles, and we do not know where to go. Most people sadly do not have the Good Shepherd to guide them. They don't recognize that only Jesus is able not only to point us to the right paths but He Himself will be with us and ride along in our journey. Jesus is there to guide our paths if only we are willing to yield to His instructions. The Bible tells us, "*There is a way that appears to be right, but in the end, it leads to death*" (Proverbs 14:12). The right approach is to yield to the Good Shepherd as our Pilot. We should allow Him to hold the steering wheel and drive our lives. God's Word, the Bible, must serve as our roadmap, and it shows us which roads to take. It tells us where to go, and it reminds us of what we expect to experience along the way. The Bible shares with us a lot of stories of people who have gone ahead of us in the race of life. Their stories inspire us, and their failures teach us valuable lessons in life. These heroes of faith serve as an encouragement and inspiration for us, and in almost all cases, they have suffered way more than whatever we are experiencing in this life, and yet, they have persevered and have stayed faithful to their Good Shepherd. In fact, we can imagine these heroes of faith cheering for us as we run the race of life. The Apostle Paul has compared our lives not just to a journey but to a race like a marathon. It's not just a game of speed like a one-hundred-meter dash, but it is a game of endurance and perseverance. He wrote that each Christian must aim to finish his or her own race. He wants us to focus on our goal and prize and not to be distracted by anything that we may encounter along the way. He wrote in his second letter to Timothy (2 Timothy 4:7), "*I have fought the good fight, I have finished the race, I have kept the faith.*" It is very important that we are always yielding to the guidance of the Good Shepherd in our life's journey. Jesus does not only know the way, or He does not merely point us in the right way; He is the Way. The Good Shepherd can see the road ahead but not the sheep. The Good Shepherd knows the best route and proper timing, that is why He can guide us along the right paths.

I remember when my family had our first road trip to California, my only guide was our car's GPS. It was a fourteen-hour drive from British Columbia, Canada, to Sacramento, California, passing through mostly unfamiliar roads. We stopped in the middle of our road trip in a small town of Medford, Oregon, and stayed overnight. It was a wonderful experience. I realized that for the duration of that trip, I relied mainly on the GPS for directions, and we arrived at my father-in-law's place with no problem. As we travel through our life's journey here on earth, there will be times when we have to go through strange places and trek on unfamiliar territories. We go through some new experiences and encounter new situations. Sometimes we just simply don't know what to do. We need guidance.

We need directions. God as our Good Shepherd has seen it all. He knows the past, the present, and even the future. The challenges that we may face as we venture into these new situations are no stranger to Him. God sent His son Jesus Christ here on earth, and He had experienced the most horrible suffering known to man, dying on the cross by crucifixion. Jesus, our Good Shepherd, knows our sufferings firsthand. He is in the best position to guide us and gives us directions when the going gets tough. When we are lost and needing guidance, we must remember what the Lord told us. We must rely on our Good Shepherd for directions in our lives. He knows what we go through in life, whether it involves going through trials and problems or celebration of victory. Jesus has been through it all.

Reflection Questions

1. Have you experienced becoming popular? How does it feel when a lot of people are tapping on your back or admiring you or giving you accolades?
2. At some point in the past, did you "step on someone else's toes" just to get ahead?
3. Are you willing to give up everything just to set things right between your soul and God?

Death Is but a Shadow

Even though I walk through the valley of the shadow of death,
I fear no evil.

—Psalm 23:4a

In the New International Version of the Holy Bible, it uses the phrase, *"Even though I walk through the darkest valley."* This particular verse is the reason why the Twenty-Third Psalm has been recited time and time again during funerals because it is oftentimes interpreted as the actual valley that a person's soul will have to pass through when he dies. It's a very scary picture of a very dark valley, with no living thing in sight and only a ghastly figure of a person's soul walking in the midst of the rough and wet road. I can picture the silhouettes of trees with no leaves and maybe with fiery eyes seen from the darkness around. We must understand that this is more of a misinterpretation of the passage. Actually, the verse does not talk about an actual death experience but only a shadow. King David was not talking here of death itself, but it is more of a "life or death" situation. A "shadow of death" or as used in other translations, the "darkest valley," means being in grave danger, just like when a flock of sheep passes through a dark valley as they move from one pasture to another. Every time the shepherd moves the flock in search of greener pasture, terrible dangers are lurking in the darkness. The enemy of the sheep is always hiding in the dark, with their eyes glowing like fire. These are lions, wolves, coyotes, or even hyenas. The role of the shepherd is very important in the sense that he is the only one who can provide real security to his flock. The sheep are not capable of protecting themselves as they are not wired with their own defense mechanism. The sheep have no match against their enemies as their enemies are strong, shrewd, and can attack them with no mercy whatsoever. The shepherd protects the flock as they move from place to place, and he does not leave his flock even though they walk in the midst of those dark valleys. The shepherd is the sheep's last line of defense.

We have to understand that after the flock of sheep has consumed a certain grassland, they have to keep on moving to find a new place. Led by the Shepherd, the flock will walk from one pasture to another, and usually, these are long hours, if not days, of traveling on foot. Along the way, they pass through narrow paths, dark valleys, and deep ravines. Oftentimes, the shepherd walks in front of the flock, and the flock follows. Sometimes, the shepherd walks from behind, making sure that the flock is intact. The sheep are secured and are not afraid of the dangers that they might encounter along the way because they know the shepherd is there to protect them. Even if they see those fiery eyes gleaming in the dark as they walk through those valleys, they fear nothing because the shepherd is with them, holding his rod and staff, ready to protect them anytime. The shepherd also makes sure that not even one of his sheep will go astray or will go in a different direction. He always counts them and makes sure they are complete and no one is missing. The shepherd is always alert and always ready for whatever danger they can face along the way. Throughout their journey, sometimes the sheep eat food or drink water along the way, and they get attracted to the things that they see around them like another living thing or the colorful surroundings. Sometimes the sheep get left behind or the sheep go in a different direction. The shepherd uses the staff to pull the neck of the sheep when he goes astray so he can get them back in line and continue on with their journey. If a sheep is lost, the Shepherd goes out of his way to find the missing sheep. Jesus gave a wonderful parable about this. He said in John 15:4–6, *"Suppose one of you has a hundred sheep and loses one of them. Doesn't he leave the ninety-nine in the open country and go after the lost sheep until he finds it? And when he finds it, he joyfully puts it on his shoulders and goes home. Then he calls his friends and neighbors together and says, 'Rejoice with me; I have found my lost sheep."*

This holds true with us and with our relationship with the Good Shepherd. As we all walk or travel on our life's journey, it is inevitable that we pass through the "valley of the shadow of death." The valley of the shadow of death represents the various stages in our lives that

> There is great comfort in knowing that the Good Shepherd is there for us when we walk through those darkest valleys.

we go through, which represents the most severe troubles we experience like a mounting problem or a serious crisis. The "valley of the shadow of death" is a time of our life that we probably don't want to experience or something that we try so hard to avoid, but it's a reality that we have to face. The "valley of the shadow of death" is an experience that most of us will probably just wish we're dead because of the pain it brings. It is like a nightmare that we fear the most, and we wish that it will not happen in real life. But think about what the Bible has to say about this. There is great comfort in knowing that the Good Shepherd is there for us when we walk through those darkest valleys. We shall fear no evil because He will walk with us as we go through those dangerous places. If you are in a bad situation, experiencing trouble or crisis, do not go away from the Good Shepherd or stray far away from the flock. Do not try to go through the crisis or problem just by yourself. Remember that God placed us in His family in order to be looked after and cared for. You have to swallow your pride and acknowledge the fact that life is meant to be shared. Jesus Himself chose twelve disciples to help Him during His ministry here on earth. While we can clearly say that Jesus didn't really need any help, but He was showing us a good example of how to go through this life. If you try to do things on your own, you will become like a sheep who goes astray, and you will become a good candidate for being devoured by the enemy. What makes you think you can go through all the challenges in life alone? We always hear the saying, "There is strength in numbers." The Bible tells us in Ecclesiastes 4:12, *"Though one may be overpowered, two can defend themselves. A cord of three strands is not quickly broken."* It simply means that if we are in constant communion with fellow believers in the Lord, it will not be easy for the enemy to harm us, and we are not giving him any foothold or an advantageous position to attack us. Being part of God's family means we shall look after one another. We shall always check on people whom we haven't seen in a long time. Maybe they are passing through their life's darkest valleys. Being part of God's family, we should look after them as well. The Good Shepherd would like us to help them. He wants them to feel His love manifested through us. He wants to use us as an effective channel of His blessing toward those people who are experiencing different crises in life and are walking through the darkest valleys.

Another thought that we can learn here is, do not employ quick fixes to solve your problems. Some people want to solve their problem in an instant and just move on to the next. Some people want to solve their problem in one day, forgetting the fact that more often than not, this problem built up and developed over the years. Men are prone to this trap especially when it comes to their relationship with their wives. Whenever a wife brings up a problem to their husbands, be it simple or serious, the man's tendency is to solve the problem right away. He wants to employ quick fixes. A lot of times, marital problems develop over a period of time. It is an accumulation of simple and minor problems that one spouse encounter day by day. One day, the spouse will just burst out his or her frustrations and explode. I remember a funny story about a housewife who served a bowl of soup to her husband who came from work. The husband made a simple comment that the soup was salty. The wife suddenly burst out saying that he probably thinks she's too dumb, that he doesn't love her anymore, that she cannot stay in their marriage. She's not happy, and she was screaming and crying. The poor husband was shocked, not knowing what has happened. He thought it was just a simple comment on the soup. But like what I mentioned earlier, it's not about the soup. It's an accumulation of different issues and problems in the past.

Sadly, a lot of couples find a quick and easy solution to their marital problems. It's called divorce. It may be a quick solution, but it's costly; it's messy; and most of all, it does not glorify God. The

Bible says in Malachi 2:16 (NASB), *"For I hate divorce," says the Lord, the God of Israel."* One of the best films about marriage that I would recommend to any couple is the movie *Fireproof.* This movie was produced by a church in Albany, Georgia, called Sherwood Baptist Church through the Kendrick Brothers (Alex and Stephen) starring Kirk Cameron and Erin Bethea. God had blessed my family in the spring of 2017 when I attended my graduation from the seminary for my master's degree in theology located in the same city. We visited Sherwood Baptist, and we got to meet their senior pastor Michael Catt and Pastor Ken Bevel. God has blessed this church tremendously through this film that has touched the lives of millions of couples worldwide. During our trip to Albany, we were also able to visit some of the places featured in the film like the Albany Fire Hall No. 1. I won't forget this quote from the movie by Michael Simmons (played by Pastor Ken Bevel). He said, *"Fireproof doesn't mean a fire will never come, but that when it comes, you'll be able to withstand it."* The solution to a marital problem is not divorce. In the same manner, the solution to financial distress is not to rob money. The solution to a serious illness is not to commit suicide. While the enemy cannot read our thoughts, he can influence and affect our actions judging from our behaviors. The enemy can tell if we are lacking in our faith especially if we have problems. He can see our actions, and he can tell if our actions imply dwindling faith, then he will come in and take advantage of it. Some of the behaviors we show to the enemy and unknowingly give him foothold are: we stop praying, we stop reading God's Words, we stop attending the church, or we stop attending Bible studies. Once the enemy sees these things happening in our lives, he tempts us even more. He makes us feel that we are no longer worthy because we have been skipping church for a long time or because we have all these problems we have no right to be active again in the ministry. Always remember that if you are a true follower of God, the Holy Spirit indwells you. He (the Holy Spirit) is the reason why a Christian cannot be possessed by an evil spirit. Yes, the enemy can influence us, but the enemy cannot totally possess us. The enemy is out there waiting for us to be out of line, to be separated from the rest of the sheep and go astray. He is waiting for the perfect opportunity, and he is patiently waiting for us to make a mistake. The Bible tells us not just to keep ourselves close to the flock, but also we need to be alert at all times. We should never put our guards down. First Peter 5:8 tells us to *"keep awake! Watch at all times. The devil is working against you. He is walking around like a hungry lion with his mouth open. He is looking for someone to eat."* The devil prowls around like a roaring lion waiting for somebody to devour. The irony of it all, if we fall into the temptation of the enemy, he will also be the first one who will blame us afterward and make us feel unworthy and create that feeling of guilt inside of us. He will make us feel that once that we made a mistake, we cannot go back to the flock anymore. He will make us believe that we are no longer worthy of being part of the family of the children of God. But we must know better than that. We must be familiar with the schemes of the enemy. If we know our Good Shepherd intimately, we will always have the confidence that the Good Shepherd's specialty is to welcome back His lost sheep with open and loving arms. He specializes in reconciling sinners to God. If you have read the parable of the prodigal son in the Gospels, you probably know what I'm trying to explain. The Good Shepherd will never reject a sinner who is coming back to Him. Jesus said in Luke 19:10, *"For the Son of Man came to seek and to save the lost."* Remind yourself to stay together with the flock. Pray together, fellowship together, and read the Bible every day. Remember that there is always strength in numbers. When you serve from your heart, then you have genuine fellowship with Christ. Having a genuine fellowship with Christ also means we strive to have fellowship with His family or flock. It is important to remember that Jesus came to serve, not to be served. Being under His flock and being under His care as your Good Shepherd also means we become part of His flock, and just like our Master, we must enjoy serving one another as well.

As I had mentioned earlier, one important thing to remember in this verse, *"Even though I walk through the valley of the shadow of death,"* with the valley representing probably the toughest trials we may have ever encounter in our lives, King David made it clear that we are just walking through the valley. We are just crossing from one side to another. Whenever you are passing through your own valleys, please make sure you are in that valley on a temporary basis only and you are not supposed to take a vacation in that valley. You are not expected to build your house in the valley, probably not even a tent. Just "passing through" means you are not expected to stay in that difficult situation for a very long time. It will certainly come to pass. For most people, whenever they encounter problems and trials in life, their tendency is to stay in that situation for a very long time. Months and even years have passed by, and they are still in that valley, and they are still suffering. They cannot pass through the valley, and they cannot move on. How many people, when they get frustrated or disappointed over something or someone, they just can't move on? As emotional beings, we have the penchant to stay in the valley and have the propensity to stay miserable and defeated. No. The psalmist tells us that we just have to walk through the valley because the Good Shepherd will always be there to help us. It will come to pass, and we are bound and destined to find the greener pasture as we are led by our Good Shepherd after we walk through the valley of the shadow of death. The Apostle Paul tells us in 2 Corinthians 4:17 that *"For our light and momentary troubles are achieving for us an eternal glory that far outweighs them all."* We have to make sure that those troubles are momentary and not permanent.

This verse 4 of the Twenty-Third Psalm as discussed earlier tells us that we shall not fear *"even though we walk through the valley of the shadow of death."* But please remember that even if it talks about death itself, even if we face real death and not just a shadow, the important thing to understand is that our Good Shepherd has conquered death already. Jesus conquered death by His resurrection, and death has no power over Him. Death is probably the most feared phenomenon known to man. Almost everybody is afraid of death. Just by the thought of it gives us chills and a lot of people don't want to talk about it. Death is probably the ultimate challenge each person can ever face. Mankind tried so many things over generations in order to defy death, but no one or nothing can actually be done to avoid it. It's a reality of life. A lot of times, the reason why we fear death so much is because of our lack of knowledge about it and what happens after death. Man fears death because of the wrong notion that it is the end of everything. Hosea 4:6 tells us (the Lord speaking) that *"my people are destroyed from lack of knowledge."* On the positive side, the hope of knowing that when a believer dies, he is "absent from the body but present with the Lord" should give us a very optimistic outlook about life and even death. Jesus, our Good Shepherd, has conquered death, and He is the only One who was able to do that. The Bible tells us in 1 Corinthians 15:55–57, *"Where, O death, is your victory? Where, O death, is your sting?" The sting of death is sin, and the power of sin is the law. But thanks be to God! He gives us the victory through our Lord Jesus Christ."* If you believe in Jesus Christ and receive Him in your life as your Savior and Lord, you shall no longer be afraid to die. Death has no power over you.

I remember when our family migrated to Canada from the Philippines in 2005, it was a bittersweet decision on our part. It was bitter because we had to leave our families, relatives, and even friends behind. Some of them are in their senior years, and we know that it will not be easy for us to probably come back and visit them again. Over the years that we are living in Canada, we just hear news time and again about our relatives who passed away. We also knew when we moved to this country, our children will grow up without getting to know much about their relatives, like their cousins and other loved ones. It will be difficult for them to grow up being really close with our relatives because of distance. I also had to give up a very generous job of being a general manager in a credit card business of a petroleum company. It was sweet because we get the opportunity to start a new life with the prospect of looking forward to a better future for our children. Migrating to a foreign land is also both exciting and scary. Exciting in the sense that we get to experience a different way of life, with new places to see, new friends to make, and a new culture to experience. It was scary especially in the beginning in the sense that there were a lot of uncertainties. There were a lot of things that we don't know, and we only had to rely on some information and experiences from other people. But sometimes, people experience things differently and see things in different ways. For somebody who had a successful career in the Philippines, moving to a new country meant that I had to start anew. I remember my first job in Canada wherein I only lasted for two days was to clean at night in a major university. It was very physically draining, and I almost fainted out of exhaustion on my second night. My second job was with a bank processing center, which was actually similar to what I did in the Philippines fifteen years earlier. I am still thankful up to now that I got that job because not too many immigrants are able to practice their professions when they arrive.

When we moved to Canada, as we bid goodbye to our families in the Philippines, they did not say they were "losing" us. You know why? They did not say they were losing us because they know exactly where we were going. They may not have a clear picture or idea about this new country that we are moving into, but they cannot say they are losing us because they know our destination. They know we are migrating to Canada. They know that we are going to an even better place. I view death as something similar to our immigration to Canada. We cannot say we are losing our loved ones who died, especially if they are believers of the Lord Jesus Christ because we know for sure where they are going. They will be absent from their bodies and present with the Lord, and this happens in an instant, the moment they die. They will go to a place of ultimate comfort and care. They will be going to a better place. They will be starting a different kind of life with God Himself.

If you are familiar with Jesus's story about the rich man and Lazarus in the sixteenth chapter of the gospel according to Luke, we know that these two men lived very different lives. The poor Lazarus has suffered all his life because of his poverty, but we can say from the story of Jesus that he was a true follower of the Lord. This was evident by his destination or the place he ended up going after he died. The rich man, on the other hand, has neglected to be a blessing to the poor beggar, and we can assume that he was not a follower of God, again based on where he ended up after he died. It was very clear from the story that when these two men died, both of them immediately went to two different places. They

Our life here on Earth is the ultimate test as to where we will spend eternity.

did not sleep in their graves as some religious groups claim. The Bible tells us that "sleeping" pertains to the body of a person who died, and it is commonly used as a metaphor for dying. The soul, on the other hand, goes to the Lord if the person is a believer. There is no such thing as "soul sleep." Lazarus, based on the story of our Lord Jesus Christ, went to what the Bible called "Abraham's bosom or paradise," which is basically what we call in our time today as "heaven." The rich man, on the other hand, went to a place of torment and agony. The Bible tells us that there is a great chasm that divides these two places, and those who are from one side cannot cross to the other side. I do not believe that the rich man went to the place of torment because he was rich. Being rich *per se* is not the issue here, and we know that there are a lot of rich people here on earth who are true followers of Jesus Christ. I believe he went the place of torment because in his life, he has not fully surrendered his life to God, and by doing so, he ignored the needs of those around him, and one of them was the poor beggar Lazarus who has been begging at his gate all his life. In this story, we debunk certain myths that we hear from many people in our time today. First, this story tells us that those who died can no longer come back to the land of the living. But what about those "ghosts" of people we know who already died? Honestly speaking, I really don't know, but what I know for sure is what the Bible tells me. A person who died can no longer come back to the land of the living. The Bible is very clear about that. Our enemy who is the prince of deception has the power to do certain things that can debilitate our faith and deceive or confuse us. While I know that God is all-powerful and He can certainly allow our dead relatives to visit us, I don't think God will contradict His word and allow that to happen. The second myth that we debunk here is that when a person dies, he goes to a temporary place while it is being decided whether he will get to heaven or hell. The Bible tells us that there is already a decision or judgment as to where a person will spend eternity the moment this person dies. Hebrews 9:27 tells us that *"just as people are destined to die once, and after that to face judgment."* This verse in Hebrew tells us that those who are alive can no longer do anything for their relatives who passed away. Our life here on Earth is the ultimate test as to where we will spend eternity. Once we die, we already lose the opportunity, so we should make the most of it while we are here. We should pass the "test" by receiving Jesus in our lives as our Lord and Savior. Once we receive Jesus in our lives, it is also expected that we share that same faith to others, especially those whom we love. It is not smart to take a big risk especially when it involves the fate of our soul for eternity. Some atheists would challenge the Christian worldview by saying that our faith in God does not make any sense at all. Some of them, if not all, hide under the guise of science and philosophy implying that Christians exercise "blind faith" and that there is no logical basis in what we believe. Here's the thing, if a person decides to follow Jesus and if it is a genuine conversion, this person will naturally produce fruit out of his faith. He will start to show love, mercy, grace; and he becomes a godly person. If for the sake of discussion, there is no life after death or there is no God like what the atheists believe, then the person who followed Christ has nothing to lose. He ended up becoming a productive member of society. But what if a person decided to be an atheist and opted to reject Christ, and again, if for the sake of discussion, there is life after death and the Christian faith is true, then this person has everything to lose. It is therefore logical and smarter to choose believing in Jesus rather than not to believe. But the truth about Jesus is not just for argument's sake. He is the one True God. He is the Good Shepherd. He is our true Savior.

When people die, their souls are in an "intermediate state" as they wait for the final resurrection wherein each one shall be given a glorified body to last for eternity. The relevance of this story to our topic of death is that for each person who dies, whether he is a true believer or not, he immediately goes to a place, either to a place of torment or to a place of comfort. If our loved ones who die are true believers, we know where they are heading to. We know that they will be with the Lord, so we do not actually lose them. In fact, if we ourselves are true

The ultimate hope is in knowing that there is a life after this life, and it gives us the motivation to move on despite all the challenges that we face in this world.

Christians, we shall see them again and be with them for eternity. For me, this is the ultimate hope that I can always hold on to. It tells me that if my natural families believe in Jesus, I will see them again. The life we have here on earth will never be completely fair, it will never be completely just, and we can never be completely comfortable. The most challenging part is knowing that one day we will all die. No matter what we do and no matter how much wealth we accumulate or credentials we achieve, one day we will meet death. Even if we don't face an accident or not succumbed to a deadly disease, one day our physical bodies will fail, and we die of old age. The ultimate hope is in knowing that there is a life after this life, and it gives us the motivation to move on despite all the challenges that we face in this world. We know that one day, there will be an end to all the sufferings and problems that we experience while living in this world. We know that all our problems will come to pass. We will not permanently be staying in that valley of the shadow of death.

Yes, indeed, death is only a shadow. While it is an inescapable reality, it does not have a permanent sting anymore to the sheep of the Good Shepherd. It is only grim reminder to Christ's followers that there was a time before we fully surrendered our lives to God when death controlled us, when death scares us, and when our only destination was eternal damnation. If you have faith in Christ and have believed in Him as your personal Lord and Savior, this is no longer the case for you, and death should not scare you anymore. Death is only a silhouette of a dark past that has been dealt with by Jesus Christ; and therefore, we must not fear death anymore. What the enemy tries to do is to pollute our minds into thinking that death is the most tragic thing that can happen to us and that death is the end of everything for us. With this lie, most people get into thinking that if life here on earth is all that there is, might as well make the most out of it, even to the point of taking advantage over others and stepping on other people's toes to get what they want the most in life. Most people unfortunately, believe in the enemy's lie that there is nothing after this life, which means our good deeds and godly acts here on earth means nothing. The reality is actually the opposite. There is undoubtedly more to this life. Death is just the crossover into beginning a new life that is entirely different from what we have right now. Death is simply a passageway to a much better situation if one is a follower of Jesus. There is nothing to be afraid about death. It's like migrating to another country, a much better one. It's a new and fresh start especially for the sheep of the Good Shepherd.

A lot of times, death becomes harder to accept by those who are left behind, by the loved ones of those who died. When my own father died about twenty years ago, it was not easy to accept. It was painful, and it devastated our whole family. The moment he died, I got to realize how important he was in my life. It would have been nice if I had spent more time with him. I moved to the city when I studied in college and then off to work. I never took an extended vacation since then. I never spent too much time with my parents after that. Usually, I would go home once a month, on the weekend. I have come home during special occasions, usually during Christmas. My father never got to see my children as he passed away before I got married. A lot of times, it seems to me that he was just there in our house. Several times in the past, when I called my mother on the phone, I would somehow look for him, forgetting that he already passed away. Probably you have experienced the same. Six months before my father died, I have seen a drastic change in his lifestyle. He stopped smoking. He stopped drinking, and he started to go to church regularly. It is my fervent hope that I get to see him again in heaven. I know that the Bible tells me that if my father has not genuinely accepted Christ in his life as his Lord and Savior, there is no chance that I can see him again. I would like to believe that he did. Same thing with my older brother and mother who passed away recently. I would like to believe that they have accepted Jesus genuinely in her heart as well.

I think the main reason why the death of a loved one becomes so painful to accept is if we are not confident whether we would see them again or not. I think our ultimate hope is being sure that there will be a time and place where we can reunite with them. For those people who belong to the family of God, those who are part of His flock, we believe and we are certain that we shall live together for eternity. It should, therefore, create a dire need for us or a great burden, if you may want to call it that way, that we must share our faith with our families and loved ones. This is the only way for us to see them again—that by sharing the gospel, they will not be just become our natural families, but they can be our spiritual families as well. When we were born into this world, God has placed us in the care of our natural families. In my case, I became part of the Carmen family. This is my natural family, and I love my family so much. But our relationship with our natural families will only last for this life-time because we can easily be separated by death. The only way for us to meet them again after they died is if our family members are included in the Lord's flock. This is the only reason why we can have the chance of seeing them again.

As I was writing this chapter, I just came back from visiting a nineteen-year-old girl who was in a coma for a few days in the hospital. She is a daughter of a single mother, and this girl was only being kept alive for several days by life-support machines. I learned that any time these life-support machines will be pulled out. It is mind-blowing to think how can a person, so young and has a full life ahead of her, be in that condition. How can we understand why a God who is all-loving and all-powerful allow those things to happen? How can our Good Shepherd let this terrible thing happen to one of His sheep? I think this is one of the most challenging questions that every Christian especially our children can ever face in our time today. We have seen a lot of bad or even evil things going on around us. Skeptics, agnostics, or even atheists pose this very difficult ques-tion to somebody who is trying to share the Gospel. How can an all-loving and all-powerful God allow bad and evil things to happen in this world? They say if God is all-loving, He would defeat evil and not allow bad things to happen, especially to good and honest people.

They say if God is all-powerful, He could defeat evil anytime He wants to, but still, evil is everywhere. Most of us have witnessed at least on television the World Trade Center bombings in New York or the senseless shooting in Las Vegas or even natural disasters like the tsunami in Japan or the typhoons in the Philippines. Their argument is that if God would not defeat evil, then He is not all-loving, and if

God could not defeat evil, then He is not all-powerful. So God can just either be all-powerful or all-loving or maybe simply He is not or maybe there is really no God. I think the answer is not whether or not evil is everywhere or not whether bad things happen especially to good people. There are certainly evil things around us, and we cannot deny it. It's a known fact and an undeniable reality. We also cannot deny that "bad" things happen to good people. We see people who are always fair, just, kind, and nice all their lives; and they even serve in the church, but then all of a sudden, something terrible happens to them or to their loved ones. We have read the Bible or even through history books that the disciples of Jesus Christ died miserably. They were severely persecuted by their enemies and had lived in dire poverty all their lives. We have seen what happened to Job in the Old Testament. I put the word *bad* in quotation because I believe from what the Bible is saying, there is nothing really bad that can happen to a child of God. It may seem bad from our perspective, but in God's divine plan and purpose, everything happens for a reason, and everything is for our own good. So how do we answer the skeptics, the agnostics, and the atheists? The answer is, we don't know the mind of God. What I believe is that it's not that God could not defeat evil but because God has decided in His infinite wisdom that He would not defeat evil *yet*. We are not always privy to His greater plans. It is a privilege sometimes to know His will, but He is not obligated to make it known to us. All we know is that all these evil or bad things are allowed by God for the time being, but we know from Bible that He will certainly put an end to all evil in this world in a time known only to Him. I like how the Apostle John puts it in the book of Revelation. Chapter 21:4 tells us, "*He will wipe every tear from their eyes. There will be no more death' or mourning or crying or pain, for the old order of things has passed away.*"

Even the death of this nineteen-year-old girl is definitely not the end of her. She is just crossing from this life to another life. Her single mother certainly did not lose her. I believe she will be with her again. Her friends did not lose her. If her death has been used by God to open the hearts of her friends and make them realize that they need Jesus in their lives, then one day she will be reunited with her friends. I believe that since this girl and her mother are both believers, they will definitely be reunited. This time nothing can ever separate them. Because of Jesus Christ, death has no sting over this young lady anymore. Because of the Good Shepherd, death has no sting over anyone of us who trust only the name of Jesus. Death is only a shadow, and we shall not fear death at all, and we praise our loving and Good Shepherd for conquering death once and for all.

This psalm also tells us that as we walk through the valley of the shadow of death, we shall fear no evil. The Good Shepherd does not want us to feel afraid of the enemy, the devil. He assured us in 1 John 4:4, *"You, dear children, are from God and have overcome them, because the one who is in you is greater than the one who is in the world."* If we have Jesus Christ in our lives, the enemy has no way to conquer or overpower us because the Holy Spirit lives or indwells in us. We should not have that defeated mentality, but instead, we must realize that Jesus has already won the victory at the cross in Calvary. We should remember that we are victorious in Christ and not victims, and so there is really nothing to fear. The enemy can only scare us or pollute our minds, but if he sees that we are confident in our positions being children of God, he will not dare touch us. God will send His angels to protect us from the evil one. The Good Shepherd will not allow the lions, hyenas, and coyotes to devour His flock, so we shall not fear those enemies out there. By being scared all our lives, the enemy can deprive us of experiencing true joy while being here on earth. By being afraid, he can prevent us from becoming more productive in the ministry. It will shift our focus away from things that would glorify God, and it will certainly make our lives miserable. We should not give the enemy a foothold in our lives that will lead us to fear him. I believe it was Martin Luther who said, *"You cannot keep birds from flying over your head but you can keep them from building a nest in your hair."* We cannot control what the enemy will try to do to attack us, but we can certainly take control of how we shall react to the enemy's temptation. We certainly can have the right resolve to run away from the

> **By being scared all our lives, the enemy can deprive us of experiencing true joy while being here on earth.**

enemy's temptation by being firm, and by having complete trust and confidence in our Good Shepherd.

Growing up in a small town in the Philippines, I have attended a lot of funerals for mostly our relatives, and you'll be surprised to know that there were a lot of superstitious beliefs about death and about the afterlife. We hear people saying that it will not hurt if they follow those superstitious beliefs and traditions. They are also very careful not to offend especially the older people. But I think going through the motion or practicing traditions that have no apparent basis in the Scripture is dangerous as it undermines, first and foremost, our faith in the Good Shepherd. I remember some of these beliefs vividly in my mind, and when I was young, I kept on questioning my parents and older siblings about it. I also got to experience these things when my father passed away. I remember meeting some people who are afraid during funerals. Some don't even want to look at the body of the deceased person. This is because they are not well informed about the true nature of death. I remember some old folks were telling us not to take a bath for the duration of the wake. They told us not to sweep the floor, make sure the coffin is facing the right direction, make sure the children have been passed over the coffin, and a lot of other things. I also remember that there are certain dishes that cannot be prepared. I have also attended the funeral services of other families. There were toy cars, toy houses, characters of people, toy money—which are all made of paper—and they believe that the dead person needs all these material things in the afterlife. One funny experience I remember was when somebody asked what are those toy characters of people represent, and we learned they were actually representing the "housemaids" of the dead person. They believe that in the afterlife, the dead person can still have a housemaid if they put a toy character representing housemaids in the dead person's coffin. The housemaids of the deceased were all afraid that one of them shall follow the dead person. They also put money, pieces of jewelries, and so many other things in the dead person's coffin.

The Bible tells us in 1 Timothy 6:7 that *"we brought nothing into the world, and we can take nothing out of it."* All these beliefs have no biblical basis, and we must discount these ideas whenever we have the chance. On the bright side, attending funerals also provide us with a good opportunity to share the love of Christ. When a person dies, most of his or her loved ones are more open to knowing more about God. People are more receptive to discussions especially in the area of death and the life after. The Bible says in Ecclesiastes 7:2, *"It is better to go to a house of mourning than to go to a house of feasting, for death is the destiny of everyone; the living should take this to heart."* When people attend funerals, they get to question their own beliefs about life and death. When people attend funerals, they are reminded of how short life is and how important it is to believe in something especially that hope of a better life compared to what we have here on earth. As a minister, it breaks my heart to handle funeral services or celebrations of life. I feel much sympathy for those loved ones who were left behind. On the other hand, I thank God because of the opportunity to explain clearly to people attending the funeral a lot of things about life, death, and most importantly, to share the love, mercy, and grace of the Good Shepherd.

Next time you go through the valley of the shadow of death, think of it as a wake-up call. God is reminding you to remember Him and His promises. During those times, we just need to call upon our Good Shepherd, and we don't need to fear death no more.

Reflection Questions

1. Have you experienced losing someone you love, either through death or any other kind of separation?
2. How will you encourage someone who just lost somebody?
3. Do you still fear death?

Rod or Staff: Which One Do You Choose?

Your rod and your staff, they comfort me.

—Psalm 23:4b

Certain professions are known for their tools or gadgets. Doctors are seen to have their stethoscopes hanging around their necks. In the old days, doctors were also wearing white blazers just like a nurse who wears her white cap. An architect or engineer is usually seen with his T-Square and wearing a hard hat. A policeman wears his uniform with his gun and badge on his side. Accountants probably have their calculators and wear eyeglasses while a minister is usually seen with his Bible and sometimes along with his clergy collared shirt. Shepherds, being one of the oldest profession, are also identified with some tools. These are called the shepherd's rod and staff. Rods and staffs are sometimes interchangeable terms especially in the Old Testament, but the Hebrew words actually have two different meanings. The Hebrew word for *rod* is *"sebet"* means a stick, which is part of a tree. It is also used to count the sheep in the flock. The Hebrew word for *staff* is *"mishena"*, which means "support or something to lean on." Together, the rod and staff give us a clear picture of

> **God will definitely won't have any second thoughts in using His shepherd's rod to discipline His people whom He loves.**

a shepherd whom we can trust for our care and protection. The Bible tells us in Numbers 17:8 (NIV) that Aaron had a staff, which *"had budded, blossomed and produced almonds,"* while in the King James Version talks about his rod, which originates from the Hebrew word *"matteh"* meaning "staff, branch, or shaft." However, the more common interpretation shows that these tools are slightly different from each other. What was interesting about Aaron's rod and Moses's staff is because these are miraculous items that God used for when He was about to free Israel from their bondage in Egypt. Moses's staff was turned by the Lord into a snake. This is to demonstrate God's awesome power to Moses who had very low self-confidence during the time God was asking him to confront the Pharaoh in Egypt and to lead the Israelites to freedom. This same staff was lifted up by Moses where God had divided the Red Sea to let the Israelites cross over. Aaron's rod, on the other hand, turned into a snake before Pharaoh in his court in Egypt. It was also used by God to turn the water in Egypt into blood. These miraculous pieces of wood had given so much hope and motivation for the people of Israel as these tools were used by God to show His power against those who took advantage of His chosen people. Aaron's rod, which represented the tribe of Levi, had sprouted and produced ripe almonds, which clearly demonstrated God's power to create, thereby putting an end to Israelites' grumblings. Pieces of Aaron's rod was actually contained as one of those few items inside the *Ark of the Covenant* as a permanent reminder and warning to God's people who keep on rebelling against Him. God will definitely won't have any second thoughts in using His shepherd's rod to discipline His people whom He loves.

The rod and staff may look plain and ordinary, but they have produced extraordinary miracles solely because we know they have been used by an extraordinary God. The Good Shepherd specializes in making use of ordinary things and achieves extraordinary victories. Since the time of Moses and Aaron, their rod and staff have always symbolized the miracles that God has performed toward the Israelites. The rod and staff have also symbolized disobedience and stubbornness. In the book of Numbers 20:8, the Lord gave specific instructions to Moses: *"Take the staff, and you and your brother Aaron gather the assembly together. Speak to that rock before their eyes and it will pour out its water. You will bring water out of the rock for the community so they and their livestock can drink."* However, probably because of too much pressure from the grumbling crowd, Moses raised his arm and struck the rock twice with his staff. Water gushed out, and the community and their livestock drank. But the Lord was not pleased with him. He said in verse 12, *"Because you did not trust in me enough to honor me as holy in the sight of the Israelites, you will not bring this community into the land I give them."* Moses himself lost the opportunity to go to the promised land because of his disobedience.

The rod and staff are also symbols of authority. It tells the flock that the shepherd holding the rod and staff has authority over the flock. He has the authority not just to lead them, but he also has the responsibility to protect them. It is human nature that sometimes we get challenged more whenever we need to submit to authorities. Some people actually don't like authorities, but since time immemorial, God has established authorities and governments to rule over His people. It is also human nature that sometimes when somebody is given or handed over some form of power to govern others, the person in authority sometimes tend to become too abusive. This is probably the reason why the line of Uncle Ben Parker in the movie *Spider-Man* became too famous when he said, "With great power comes great responsibility." Sometimes, authorities are abusive as we can read and even witness throughout history that there have been several governmental authorities, a line of kings and emperors, and even religious leaders who committed inhuman atrocities and all forms of dictatorship. They cannot handle the power and authority handed over to them. Instead of humbling themselves and serving their subjects true to their hearts, the power goes right into their heads, and they start to abuse and work against the very people who supported them in those positions. They start enriching themselves at the expense of their subjects and making dishonest gains. This is the reason why God needs to impose discipline and corrections not just among His flock but also to its leaders. If He just lets us do what we want to do, like sheep, we will definitely go astray. If He gives us all the freedom and leniency that we ask, we tend to abuse that freedom and do things that can eventually harm ourselves and each other. On the other hand, if He lets us be subjected to governing authorities, some authorities abuse their power and oppress those under them. The Good Shepherd just gives us enough of both because more often than not, we do not know what is really good for us. Being under someone else's authority here on Earth creates a humbling attitude for each one of us. Submitting to authorities provide accountability, and without accountability, we become irresponsible and uncooperative. Yes, we are the sheep of the Good Shepherd. We are citizens of heaven, and we are the children of God Almighty, but we still need to submit to earthly authorities while we are still living in this world. The Scripture talks about submission to authority in Romans 13:1, *"Let everyone be subject to the governing authorities, for there is no authority except that which God has established. The authorities that exist have been established by God."* It did not say that all these authorities are godly. God institutes these authorities, but just like how He gives free will to each individual, the same freedom of choice is given to rulers of nations and even leaders of church congregations. If you read stories of the kings of Israel and Judah in the Old Testament, you will see that there were godly and ungodly kings. It all boils down to which path they chose to follow.

The Lord Jesus Christ, our Good Shepherd, walked here on earth in a time and place when one of the most brutal empires was ruling the land, the Romans. Despite the abuse and cruelty that He experienced under the Roman rule and unfortunately, under the Jewish leaders, Jesus modeled perfect submission to governing authorities. He did not lead any rebellion against the governing power. He did not incite anything that will topple down Rome. He humbly submitted to their rulings and obey the laws of the land, no matter how unfair it turned out and how abusive they have become. One time, the Pharisees tried to trap Him into saying something against Rome. They asked Him regarding His opinion on whether to pay the imperial tax to Caesar or not. Our Good Shepherd knows what goes on inside man's heart and mind. He knew that the Pharisees were trying to trap Him. What He said afterward amazed everyone. He said in Matthew 22:19–22, *"Show me the coin used for paying the tax.' They brought him a denarius, and he asked them, 'Whose image is this? And whose inscription?' 'Caesar's,' they replied. Then he said to them, 'So give back to Caesar what is Caesar's, and to God what is God's.' When they heard this, they were amazed. So they left him and went away."* I understand that sometimes it is really hard to submit to authorities, like the government, to our boss in the office, to our pastor in the church, to our teacher in school and sometimes, even wives are having a hard time submitting to their husbands. God wants to develop our character especially in the area of humility that is why He wants us to submit to authorities. There is also a practical benefit in submitting to authorities. Generally, we won't get into trouble if we are obedient.

There was a time in the history of the Israelites when they were not being ruled by any king particularly after God has rescued them from their slavery in Egypt. At one point, the Israelites have requested for a king from the Lord through the prophet Samuel. Because of their stubbornness, the Lord granted them their request with the stern warning as to how a king, if he turns out to be wicked and disobedient, would oppress them and take everything they own. 1 Samuel 8:6–11,

> *But when they said, "Give us a king to lead us," this displeased Samuel; so he prayed to the Lord. And the Lord told him: "Listen to all that the people are saying to you; it is not you they have rejected, but they have rejected me as their king. As they have done from the day I brought them up out of Egypt until this day, forsaking me and serving other gods, so they are doing to you. Now listen to them; but warn them solemnly and let them know what the king who will reign over them will claim as his rights.*

However, the people were stubborn and still wanted to have a king just like their neighboring countries, so God granted their request. God then chose King Saul as the very first king of Israel. Sometimes, God will let us get what we want even if it will not be "good" for us. It will not be "good" in a sense that we'll experience hardship because of what we asked from the Lord, but that is His way of teaching us a lesson in life. It will still be good for us in the long run if we learn from such experience and learn how to trust God even more in the future.

Throughout the history of God's chosen people and after the death of King David and later on King Solomon, we have seen that different kings have come and gone after the nation was divided into the northern (Israel) and southern (Judah) kingdoms. Most are wicked, some are partly good, and a few were godly. King Ahab of Israel topped the list as the worst king up to his time.

Sometimes, God will let us get what we want even if it will not be "good" for us.

He reigned from 874–853 BC. The good kings were mostly in Judah. They are King Asa, King Jehosaphat, King Hezekiah, and King Josiah. Even in modern times and during our time today, we see country presidents who are dictators, and abusive but God uses these rulers to accomplish His divine purposes. During the time of the Israelites, He even used certain kings to punish His own people, like King Nebuchadnezzar. Proverbs 21:1 tells us, *"In the* LORD's *hand the king's heart is a stream of water that he channels toward all who please him."* The Good Shepherd is the complete opposite of all these abusive kings that we have seen or read throughout history. He is the King of kings and Lord of lords, but He was never abusive. He came to serve and not to be served. He does not lord over nor take advantage of His subjects or asked them to give up their lives, but instead, He actually did the opposite: He gave His life for His sheep!

Rods are used both as defensive and even offensive weapons. It is also used as a walking stick for the shepherd. The rod is primarily used for protection against the wild beasts as it is not unusual for the shepherd to face terrible dangers for his sheep. The Bible tells us that King David, when he was still a shepherd looking after his father's flock, had fought lions and bears to protect his sheep. It could have cost him his life a couple of times, but he knew that was his main responsibility. This is the primary use of the shepherd's rod—as an offensive weapon to protect the flock. Of course, during those times, there were no stun guns, rifles, or bear sprays. All these good old-fashioned shepherds had to rely on was a shepherd's rod. It has to be strong and shouldn't easily break. It should be made from any kind of strong and fine piece of wood. Likewise, the rod is not only used by the shepherd to protect the flock; the same rod is also used to chastise or discipline a wayward or stubborn sheep. The Bible tells us that "*a rod and a reprimand impart wisdom*" (Prov. 29:15), and this is basically what the Good Shepherd will do to us if we are stubborn or hardheaded as well. He needs to use his rod to discipline the sheep under His authority. It is interesting to note that King David, the author of the Twenty-Third Psalm, with his background as a shepherd, also used the rod metaphor in his covenant with the Lord found in 2 Samuel 7:14 (KJV), "*I will be his father, and he shall be my son. If he commits iniquity, I will chasten him with the rod of men, and with the stripes of the children of men.*"

Discipline is a very vital part of any person's life. Somebody who grew up without being disciplined by his parents will most likely have an unruly or wayward personality. The Bible stresses that God disciplines whom He loves. Parents who discipline their children also prove that they don't want them to turn out as a stubborn person because they love their children. The Bible has a lot to say about this, with the rod symbolizing discipline. Proverbs 13:24 (NIV) says, "*Whoever spares the rod hates their children, but the one who loves their children is careful to discipline them.*" The role of the shepherd is the same. If he has a sheep that is stubborn and is giving him a headache, sometimes it is necessary to use the rod to discipline the problematic sheep. If the shepherd really loves his flock, he will not allow one sheep to become a troublemaker. He would use his rod to correct this particular sheep for its own sake and also for the sake of the rest of the flock. A stubborn sheep is like a rotten apple in a basketful of good ones. Something has to be done to that rotten apple so it won't "infect" the whole basket.

King David himself experienced being chastised by God with His "rod" of discipline when he committed some terrible sins in his life. He committed adultery with the wife of one of his loyal army officers, and he was also responsible for the death of such officer. King David did not escape God's rod of discipline. I believe one of the reasons why King David was called a "man after God's own heart" is not because he was a holy or a "good boy" through and through, like a teacher's pet in an elementary school or like that highly efficient employee in a company. He was not that type who wouldn't hurt a fly, so to speak, and it is not because he never committed any serious booboo in his life. God was pleased with King David's life because in spite of his iniquities and failures, and of course, the terrible consequences he faced because of those sins, King David still clung on to the Good Shepherd. His faith did not falter, and he was able to

> Whenever we see or experience God's rod, we must remember that the same rod He uses for our protection is the same rod He will use to discipline us when necessary.

move on and recovered from his situation. He learned his lesson the hard way, but he was able to turn around and changed his life for the better. God will call us a "man (or woman) after His heart" not because we won't give Him any headache at all throughout our lives. Remember that we are all sinners, and we all fall short of His glory. No one is righteous. But God will be impressed with our lives, and He will give us another chance if He sees that after we stumble and fall, we shall completely rely on Him and be able to stand up and continue on with our life's journey. He will welcome us with open arms if He sees that we have learned our lesson, maybe in a hard way; but after that, we have the resolve to do better next time.

The shepherd used the rod to protect his flock from the enemies. Every flock of sheep has enemies. These are predators like wolves, lions, and bears who are lurking in the dark waiting for someone they can devour. The shepherd is always alert and prepared to use his rod whenever necessary to protect his flock. A sheep seeing the rod in possession of his master reminds him of two things—*discipline and protection.* This is very important as we picture the Good Shepherd in our lives. Whenever we see or experience God's rod, we must remember that the same rod He uses for our protection is the same rod He will use to discipline us when necessary. We should not be afraid of God's rod. As part of His flock, we must understand that the rod is there for our benefit. God is not a ruthless dictator or a merciless ruler. He is our Good Shepherd. If He uses the rod to discipline us, we can rest assured that it will be good for us and it will be for our benefit. We must not be afraid of the Shepherd's rod because it becomes a part of our lives. When we see the rod often, we experience its protection often and its discipline probably more often. It's a symbolism that our Good Shepherd will always be there to protect us from our enemies and to discipline us when we become stubborn and difficult to handle.

Another tool that the shepherd uses is the staff. A shepherd's staff is an important but another primitive tool that the shepherd uses. It is also called a crook. Like the rod, the staff also symbolizes authority. It gives the shepherd a longer "arm" and reach. Waving the staff with an outstretched arm helps the shepherd to block off and steer the sheep in the direction he wants them to go. It guides their direction. Sometimes, when the flock starts moving from one place to another, the sheep would fall into the cliff, and the shepherd will use the staff to pull them up. The staff's hook facilitates the recovery of fallen animals by pulling them by their neck or leg. For me, the staff is as significant as the rod. Based on the information we earlier gathered about the sheep, we know that they have the tendency to go astray or walk in a different direction. Sheep can easily be distracted by almost anything that they see along the way and walk toward a different path away from the flock. The Bible has something to say about this. Comparing us to the sheep, the prophet Isaiah wrote, *"We all, like sheep, have gone astray, each of us has turned to our own way; and the LORD has laid on him the iniquity of us all"* (Is. 53:6). The sheep has the tendency to go on his own way, that is why the Shepherd needs his staff to draw us back and pull our necks if necessary so He can steer the sheep back toward the right direction of the entire flock.

The Christian life is like that journey being made by the flock, and just like any other journey, sometimes we go astray or wayward; we have that tendency to go in a different direction. We have the propensity to follow the ways of the world or the lure of the flesh. The Bible says in 1 John 2:16, *"For everything in the world—the lust of the flesh, the lust of the eyes, and the pride of life—comes not from the Father but from the world."* It is in our nature to drift away from the Shepherd. Sometimes it seems that our relationship with the Good

Shepherd is too precarious, and we easily drift apart and break His commandments. The more we run away from Him, or from His flock, the more we run the risk of getting lost, and at some point, we may even forget our way back to Him. We wake up one day, and we are lost. This happens to us especially if we hear so many directions and even nonchalant pieces of advice from different people. If our lives are not quiet enough to just listen to the word of the Good Shepherd, then it is easy for us to be misled or even misunderstood God's instruction, and we end up heading toward the wrong direction. This is where the staff of the Good Shepherd comes into play. Our Good Shepherd has to pull our neck sometimes so He can get us back in line. Symbolically, He uses His staff do this. Do you feel your neck aches sometimes? Do you feel that sometimes you go into a certain direction but it seems so hard and yet you still exert too much effort and it seems there is a force trying to pull you back and steer you to a different direction? I believe that is God's staff. Sometimes God, our Good Shepherd, has to do that to us. He pulls our neck with His invisible staff so we don't go astray, and He doesn't mind if our neck hurts a little. We need that feeling to wake up from our illusions. He pulls us because He does not want us to go on our own, but instead, He always desire for us and to walk along with the rest of the flock. Fortunately, we have a Good Shepherd who knows where we should go and where we should not go. He can see what is going on in the dark, on the wrong path out there. He knows what He is doing. He is familiar which each and every way we want to go. If you feel the slight pull of God's staff, you better follow and let go of your own personal agenda and let the Good Shepherd steer you back in the right direction. It is a blessing to feel the staff of God pulling us back in the right direction. It only means the Good Shepherd cares for us and wants us to trek on the right paths. If we can just go to any place we want—sometimes even directions that clearly bring us into trouble—and if we don't feel anything, we have to think about it and examine our relationship with God seriously. Are we truly part of God's flock? Is He our Good Shepherd? Are we sure about this? Sometimes, we think we know what we're doing, we think we know where we're going, but oftentimes, we don't; and we are heading for destruction. If you don't want God to pull your neck with His staff, stay in line and stay with the flock. Follow His direction. It is for your benefit. Just like the sheep, we can easily get distracted if we look to the left or to the right and not focused on the Shepherd. But you know there is danger waiting for us out there. Just like in those valleys, a lot of enemies are waiting for the sheep to be separated from the flock. There's foxes, coyotes, and lions. The Good Shepherd knows what is going to happen if He allows us to go on our own way. The enemy is back there, hiding in the dark like a ferocious wolf or other wild animals waiting for the right opportunity to harm us. The enemy prowls like a roaring lion looking for someone to devour. He is looking for a sheep that will go astray. He is out there waiting to steal, kill, and destroy. During those times when we face terrible dangers, Jesus our Good Shepherd is there to comfort us with His rod and staff.

I probably belong to a generation where it was normal for our parents to spank their children when we were young. I grew up not just getting spanked by my parents but even by my teachers in elementary school as well. It was common during those years especially I grew up in a small town in a third-world country. Getting spanked with our father's belt or our mother's slippers or our teacher's measuring rod is not unusual for us kids during those times. I remember when I was in grade two, we were supposed to write our names on five sheets of paper every day. If ever we miss a page or two in any day, we get spanking from our teacher equivalent to the number of papers we missed. All we need is to miss it once, and after we experienced getting spanked, we always made sure we had all those five sheets of paper all prepared every day with our names nicely written on those papers. I know that these kinds of practices are no longer tolerated in this generation, but to be honest, there were good and important disciplines learned with those kinds of practices. My siblings and I did not have to reach that point of having our parents really spank us. Most of the time, by their mere words, we would obey already. A lot of times, we won't push them to their limits. We know that if we do that, we will get the spanking we deserve, and we will for sure, regret it. For most times, my father's leather belt hanging behind the door is a good enough reminder for all of us that he is always ready to impose discipline. Just by the sight of that belt alone scares me enough to make me obey what he wants me to do. I remember we did a similar thing with our daughter. We hanged a spanking rod near our bedroom door and named it Spanky. It served as a reminder to her that we will have to use Spanky when necessary to discipline her. I don't remember using it at all, and we thank God for our children.

Another pastor once told me that we should actually be glad if we feel the discipline being imposed on us by the Good Shepherd. I asked him why, and his explanation was simple, and yet it opened my mind to a whole new dimension of discipline. He said, when God disciplines us, He has a good reason for doing so. Sometimes, the Good Shepherd "hits" us with His disciplining rod. He hits us so hard that we feel like getting so broken. When God disciplines us with His rod, it only tells us that He is there watching us and wanting us to correct our ways. He does not want us to go astray. When a shepherd strikes his sheep, it simply means that the sheep are not behaving in a way it is supposed to behave. God does the same to us. When we don't behave in a way that He expects us to behave or when we don't live our lives in a way that He expects us to live our lives, He will need to discipline us with His rod and staff of correction. It will hurt us for sure, and we need that hurt in our lives. We need to feel it, if you are familiar with the saying, "No pain, no gain." We must be more scared if we are doing ungodly things, and despite all that, we seem to get away with it; and all things seem to be well with our lives, and it seems that God is not exercising any discipline. We must be more scared because probably we are not part of His flock in the first place. This is a more serious problem. No responsible father will allow his children to behave in an unacceptable manner without disciplining them. A truly loving father will not allow his child to continue in his wrong ways and difficult attitude. He will definitely do something to get his child's attention. God's discipline is interpreted in two ways:

> No responsible father will allow his children to behave in an unacceptable manner without disciplining them.

First, it may not necessarily be a discipline in itself, but instead, it can be a test. He gives us tough situations, and He lets us go through trials and hardships because He wants to test us. He wants us to prove to Him that we'll stay under His care no matter what. He wants us to show Him that He is still first in our lives, just like what we usually say or profess with our mouths. This happens to Job in the Old Testament. He received all kinds of beatings and trials in his life but not because there was something that needed to be corrected in him; he was made the subject of a cosmic battle between God and Satan. He was put into a test, and by God's grace, Job passed the test with flying colors. Second, God's discipline would normally arise or necessitated by our previous actions. These are called chastisements as it represents the consequences of our past sins and negative actions. God had to chastise us or "spank" us if necessary because we are stubborn and because of what we did. God knows that if He doesn't do that, we will for sure do it again and maybe even worse the second time. God is a just God. He will not let us get away that easy. He needs to teach us a lesson even if it's for the second time or the third time until we learn our lesson, and it is for our own benefit. God knows that it is in our nature to take control and do things our way. Since God loves us so much, He will not allow us to go astray. Like a shepherd, He pulls our neck with His staff and hits us with His rod of correction. If He totally allows us to go on our own, He knows that we will not end up in green pastures beside quiet waters, but instead, we will be heading toward the pit of destruction; maybe even worse, we fall into the hands our enemies.

If you are a parent like me, you know that it breaks your heart to discipline your child sometimes. It is normal for a child to be stubborn or to disobey us, parents. In a Christian context, it is called sinning. Whenever our children disobey us, they still remain to be our children. Their last names are still the same. They are still part of our family, and nothing can ever change that. However, as responsible parents, my wife and I need to discipline them. We need to be a bit harsh on them sometimes. Not because we do not love them anymore because of his offense but because we love them so much that we want them to learn from their mistakes. Sometimes it may require us to suspend some of our children's privileges like playing video games or watching TV, but we just had to do it even if it means seeing them sad for a while. It breaks the heart of a parent to discipline their children, but they just need to do it.

I used to be a professor of accounting subjects at a university in the Philippines. Since I taught in the evening, most of my students had work during the day. Most of them had degrees already but decided to pursue accounting in order to qualify for other positions in their work or even get promoted. There was one student of mine who was very smart. He was very friendly to me and friendly to his classmates. In fact, he already knew most of the lessons, and he learned most of it from his actual office experience during the day. He would always help me even check test papers, and he is what some would call "teacher's pet." But I like this student. He was always a step ahead of his classmates, and like what I said earlier, he knew most of the lessons already. As the term went on, I noticed that he was slowly getting more and more complacent with his course. He was always late, had lots of absences, and his grades slowly dwindled down. I talked to him several times, but he seemed to get even more complacent and arrogant, telling me that he already knew everything that I can teach him in that program, so he didn't even want to attend the lectures. He just wanted to come to class to take exams. At the end of the semester, I gave the class individual projects to work on, and it was part of their final grade. He was too lazy to work on his own project, and I learned that he borrowed his classmate's project and just copied it. What's worse, he submitted both of their projects very late. While I can easily pull his grades up, I knew I had to give him a failing mark. He was the only one during that school term that got a failing mark under my classes. It saddened me to do it because after all, he was not just a student but also a friend. I needed to discipline him, and hopefully, he learned from that experience. He cried when he learned about his failing grade, and he came to me asking why. This time he realized how important for him to pass my subject. After I explained everything including details and examples of my disappointments over his behavior, he was devastated and sincerely apologized to me. He said it was a lesson he will never forget, and I really hope he won't. He said he may have failed my subject, but he definitely learned something else more valuable as he moved on with his life.

The Good Shepherd will never intend to harm His flock. He has their best intentions in His mind. However, there are certain things that He needs to do sometimes mainly because of His flock's behavior. I had always wondered how God must have felt when Jesus Christ died on the cross because of our sins. I know everyone will agree with me that as God's children and part of His flock, it is right for the Good Shepherd to discipline us when we are stubborn especially when we are sinning. But the case of Jesus Christ is different. It doesn't make sense to me. He did not sin, and yet God had Him go through all kinds of sufferings for each one of us. God knows that the ultimate discipline that we deserve as sinners is something that will last forever (i.e., we are bound to spend eternity in hell). As a Good Shepherd and a loving God, He does not want each one of us to end up in hell; He does not want that to happen to any one of us. We can never understand how God must have felt when He made the decision to let Jesus suffer and die on the cross. I can understand dying for somebody I love or for somebody who is a good person. Any father would probably not hesitate to die for his own family, but for someone to die so that His enemy can be saved, this is something we can never understand. As sinners, we are considered the enemy of God, but Romans 5:8 tells us, "*But God demonstrates his own love for us in this: While we were still sinners, Christ died for us.*" We were God's enemy because we are sinners and He is holy, but nevertheless, God sent His Son Jesus Christ to die for us. How can we not accept the discipline of our Good Shepherd? How can we not welcome His rod and staff to be used for us when He Himself did not spare His own Son to die on the cross for us in order that we may have everlasting life? The least we can do is to accept His discipline whenever He wants to impose it because we know that we desperately need it. The least we can do is be grateful for everything that He has done and has been doing in our lives.

Even in the church, one of the most difficult things to do especially if you are the pastor is to impose discipline toward your members. It is in every man's nature to resist any kind of discipline. In general, we feel offended when someone else rebukes us or points out our mistakes and wrongdoings. Much more if that someone has authority over us to impose certain disciplines. People often confused discipline against love. Oftentimes, only the best of friends can really tell each other what needs to be said, be it a compliment or a rebuke. A person in authority, in a church for example, takes a considerable risk whenever discipline needs to be imposed because the usual tendency of the person being disciplined is to leave the church and just start again somewhere, but if this is always the case, the person never learns his lesson, and chances are, the person will commit the same mistakes over and over again. The person imposing the discipline must also be very careful; and he or she must always exhibit humility, impartiality, and most of all, love. Other people use their authority to discipline others or lord over other servants in the church, and God was very clear about His dislike over these kinds of leaders. The apostle Peter reminds us in 1 Peter 5:2–4, *"Be shepherds of God's flock that is under your care, watching over them—not because you must, but because you are willing, as God wants you to be; not pursuing dishonest gain, but eager to serve; not lording it over those entrusted to you, but being examples to the flock. And when the Chief Shepherd appears, you will receive the crown of glory that will never fade away."* We have seen many times how power or authority has corrupted the minds of leaders; the church is no exception. I have seen politics not just in the corporate world but also in the church, and this is a sad reality. If you are a church leader, especially as a pastor or shepherd, you must be very careful about this because one thing is for sure: the Chief Shepherd will one day come and will make you accountable for everything that you have done. Sometimes church leaders hide under the guise of a biblical passage to pursue dishonest gain or undue influence over the other workers or volunteers in the church. There is a very thin line that divides a true from a false shepherd, and for most people, they don't see it since both of them appear the same in the outside. But God knows what is going on in the inside, and He has warned us that there will be false shepherds or even wolves in sheep's clothing. God sees the heart of every man. A false servant, a wolf in sheep's clothing, can fool each one of us but certainly not God. It will just be a matter of time when God will expose this person and save His flock.

The idea of discipline is probably one of the toughest principles that we must live by especially in the church. It's hard to implement if you are the person in authority and it's hard to accept if you are the person being disciplined. But I think the best way to fully understand it is to go back to the discipline that was perfectly illustrated by Jesus Christ, our Good Shepherd. A leader of the flock must know how to practice what he preaches. If a pastor knows how to impose discipline, he must also be willing to be disciplined if it reaches that point. Our Good Shepherd suffered all those kinds of punishment, not because of His own wrongdoing but because of our iniquities. If this reality sinks well with each one of us, it will not be difficult for us to experience the Good Shepherd's rod of correction and the staff of discipline. He is always willing to do that because He loves us unconditionally. He wants us to go back under His care whenever we go astray.

I will end this chapter with two important spiritual symbolisms of the rod and staff. I believe that the rod also symbolizes God's Word. The word of God is the sword of the Spirit. It gives us the ultimate protection we can ever have against the enemy. When Jesus Christ was tempted by Satan in the wilderness, He used the Word of God as His weapon. The Word of God is a powerful weapon. As part of God's flock, we must learn how to use His words. The Word of God is our weapon against everything that the enemy will put on our way. Sometimes we feel that we are not with the Good Shepherd, but we must remember that He allows us to use His rod representing His Word. However, we cannot interpret the Word of God effectively using our own wisdom. We need the Holy Spirit to help and guide us understand God's Word. I also believe that the shepherd's staff represents the Holy Spirit, and He guides us not only in reading God's Word, but He guides us throughout our life. The Holy Spirit provides comfort for each one of us. Sometimes we hear the still, small voice that refreshes our soul. Jesus Christ promised that God will send the Comforter, the Holy Spirit. He said in John 14:16 (KJV), *"And I will pray the Father, and he shall give you another Comforter, that he may abide with you for ever.*" The Good Shepherd has certainly given us the most important weapon that we can use to survive the challenges of this life, His rod, His Word. He also sends us the Holy Spirit, His staff, whom we can always lean on, whom we can always trust and rely on. He is the third person of the triune Godhead, and He represents the Good Shepherd living inside each one of us.

Reflection Questions

1. Have you ever felt going in one direction but it seems that you are being pulled away to another path?
2. Did you experience being disciplined by somebody who has authority over you?
3. What is your usual reaction when somebody rebukes you or points out your mistakes?

Behind Enemy Lines

You prepare a table before me in the presence of my enemies.
—Psalm 23:5a

In reading the Twenty-Third Psalm, you may notice that in the first three verses, King David is referring to God in the third person (the Lord, He makes, He leads, He guides, He restores). In verses 4 and 5, King David is directly communicating with his Shepherd in a more personal way (Your rod, Your staff, You prepare, You anoint). We can see here that the psalmist is becoming more and more intimate with his Good Shepherd as he goes on with this psalm. He started addressing God in the third person, but eventually, it progresses into a more intimate relationship. We are sometimes like that in our spiritual life. For some people, they get to know the Lord initially in their "heads" only. Sometimes, when someone claims that he has received Jesus Christ in his life as his Lord, it's only head knowledge. He is still undergoing a process, and this works for some people. First, they acquire enough knowledge and information about Him in their heads, but eventually, they will open up their hearts, which is important and allow their faith to develop fully. However, as we get to know the Lord day by day, He will slowly reveal Himself to us in a very personal and intimate way. At that point, we shall no longer hesitate to call Him "our" Shepherd, or "our" personal Lord and Savior. At that time, we shall no longer look at Him in the third person.

In verse 5, the psalmist basically uses other analogies in terms of his relationship with Him. If we are going to study this verse further, he compares God not just to a shepherd but to a gracious host receiving a special guest. King David compares God to somebody like his ally, probably more like a war ally who receives a friend who came from a long journey or even someone who came from the battle. We know that King David was a war hero, and he had lots of experience on the battlefield. He was not only a shepherd, a worshipper, but he was an accomplished war commander. The person who plays the harp wonderfully wrote poetic psalms and was very artistic and gifted in music is the same person who defeated the giant Goliath and killed tens of thousands of Israel's enemies in different battles.

We also have to understand the Middle-Eastern etiquette or their tradition during those times especially in Israel. Most people were desert dwellers, and they live in temporary abodes like tents. They move from place to place, and usually, one group would represent a clan, a family, or sometimes even a group of soldiers from a kingdom. Even the Israelites were desert wanderers living in tents for forty years after they escaped from Egypt. These desert dwellers usually see each other in the desert. One group sets up a tent in one area and the other group in another area that is quite far from the other, especially if they are enemies. They will set up their tents far enough especially if they are feuding clans, but it should be close enough so they can still see what the other camp is doing. They wanted to be prepared just in case the other clan is planning something bad against the other. They wanted to be sure that there are no surprise attacks from the other group. It is also common that one family who may be at odds with another family will end up setting tents that are just a stone's throw away. If another traveler or visitor passes by and comes into one of the tents, the host welcomes him graciously into his tent. Because of the hot weather or temperature in the desert, they usually put an extension or canopy outside their tents, more like a gazebo in our time today. Instead of them going inside, the host will set up the dining table under this extension area where the visitor can eat. If it so happens that the visitor is an enemy of another group, it is the host's duty and responsibility to protect him at all cost. So not only that the table will be set up in full view of the visitor's enemy, but the host is also prepared to do whatever is necessary to protect his guest just in case the visitor's enemy from the other group attacks. There is a famous old adage that goes like, "The enemy of my enemy is my friend." During these times, no one can touch the visitor for as long as he is under the roof of the gracious host. This is the picture that King David is trying to paint in this verse. When we are under the dwelling place of the Good Shepherd, we are protected from the enemy's attacks. God assures us that the One who is in us is greater than the one who is in the world." I believe there is a valuable lesson that we can learn from this setup. We cannot expect any protection from the Good Shepherd if we don't submit under His Lordship. If we belong to another flock, we cannot call Him our Shepherd at all. We have to make sure that we indeed dwell under His care and rest in the shadow of His wings. We have to make sure that whatever we do, we are always within the spiritual covering of the Good Shepherd.

> **When we are under the dwelling place of the Good Shepherd, we are protected from the enemy's attacks.**

There is a story in the Bible that talks about being a gracious host in a somewhat similar instance although this story is probably on the extreme side. Lot, the nephew of Abraham, even offered his own daughters in order to protect his visitors staying at his place. These visitors were actually angels who were sent by the Lord to destroy Sodom. This story appears in Genesis 19:1–11. The two men appeared in Sodom and stayed at Lot's place upon the latter's insistence. Lot even prepared a meal for them, and as they were about to go to bed, the wicked men of Sodom surrounded his house demanding Lot to turn over his visitors as they would like to have sex with the men. Lot begged them not to do this evil thing, and in the process, he offered up his two virgin daughters. This is one of the stories in the Bible that really gives me a difficult time to understand. Why would a father even think or try to do this heinous thing to his daughters? Why would he offer his daughters to these vicious men? But we don't really know the whole story aside from what was told in the Bible. This story tells us that in those days, being a host is a great responsibility, and he takes it seriously when somebody came to his dwelling place for refuge. Lot's action was definitely not right by offering his daughters. Some scholars say that he may just be stalling time in order to protect his visitors, but some say his offer was real. Some interpretations say that Lot believes that God will intervene on his behalf. True enough, in the end, God did not allow any of those pervert actions to happen, and He interfered Himself and protected Lot and his family.

The point that King David was trying to tell us is that his Lord is like a gracious host who welcomes him in His house. The Host prepares a warm and sumptuous meal for him. He sets up in that extension or canopy, so everyone can see him including his enemies, but they cannot do anything against him because he is under His protection.

What a very nice picture as to how God receives us in His house! What a profound illustration as to how God invites us to His dwelling place! If we dwell in the house of the Lord, we can rest assured that the enemy cannot harm us. The Gracious Host will always be there to protect us.

> Knowing that one day we shall be received by the Gracious Host in His dwelling place must give us the motivation and hope to move on and keep walking in our life's journey.

This verse also tells us that the blessing we receive from the Lord is not necessarily the absence of problems or the elimination of our enemies. The blessing here is a table prepared by God Himself in the presence of our enemies, and even in the midst of problems, we can have fellowship with Him. The table prepared by the Gracious Host is symbolic of our intimate relationship and connection with Him, and this should clearly strengthen us in the sense that in the midst of problems, trials, sufferings, and the dangers that we face and after a very long journey, under the scorching heat of the desert, we can find joy and comfort in our fellowship with the Lord. We can find joy and comfort under the roof of our Gracious Host. The long journey in the desert represents our life's journey, which is not an easy one. Knowing that one day we shall be received by the Gracious Host in His dwelling place must give us the motivation and hope to move on and keep walking in our life's journey.

For people who have surrendered their lives to the Good Shepherd, it is not unusual that there will be oppositions, or worse, we can have enemies. A lot of people will not understand what we are trying to accomplish or Who we are trying to follow. A follower of Jesus Christ is expected to do or practice things that are out of the ordinary. We are commanded to *"speak the truth in love"* and even rebuke or correct a brother or sister in faith. The Bible tells us in Romans 12:12, *"Do not conform to the pattern of this world, but be transformed by the renewing of your mind. Then you will be able to test and approve what God's will is—his good, pleasing and perfect will."* By obeying God in terms of not conforming to the patterns of this world, we end up making enemies unintentionally with people who are of this world. It will not be easy for those who are lost to understand the message that we carry and the mission that we are tasked to undertake. We expect to experience persecutions especially with regard to our faith and having enemies is something we should anticipate especially if we are truly following our Good Shepherd. We should not be surprised if we make enemies ourselves because Jesus Christ made a lot of enemies during His ministry here on earth as well, and He said in John 16:33, *"I have told you these things, so that in me you may have peace. In this world you will have trouble. But take heart! I have overcome the world."* We are not expected to feel comfortable or even feel at home in this world. The reason is because this world is not our home. We are just like those tent dwellers in the desert. We are just "passing by" *en route* to our permanent residence. We are only strangers on this planet, like foreigners or tourists but not citizens. We are not even permanent residents or "green card holders." Usually, a stranger or a foreigner is a good candidate for getting into trouble whenever he visits a foreign land. This is because a stranger does things "strangely" in comparison with the permanent residents or citizens. The stranger has a different culture, different tradition, different preferences, and sometimes even different looks. Because the stranger is different from the rest, he or she is most likely going to stand out, be noticed, offend somebody, and even end up making an enemy. We know that in this world, our ultimate enemy, who is God's main adversary, is the devil Satan along with his minions of demons or fallen angels. He is our real enemy because he takes advantage of each and every opportunity in order to make our lives difficult and cause trouble upon us. His goal is to make the lives of Jesus's followers miserable to the point that we lose the joy of our salvation and doubt our own "nationality" as God's children. He does this by tempting us in whatever we do or wherever we go. The enemy will try everything to make us "feel at home" in this world in order for us to completely forget our real nationality and who we truly are, who we truly belong to and that our citizenship actually belongs in heaven. The enemy will try to lure us into everything that this world has to offer—materialism, self-centeredness, lust, popularity, power, and other things that can drive us farther and farther away from our Good Shepherd. The enemy knows that by doing that, we shall become less and less effective in fulfilling our true purpose here on earth in following His will. By being so "at home" in this world, we can forget why God has placed us here in the first place. If the enemy succeeds, we lose our joy throughout this life, and we lose our rewards and crowns in the life to come.

I remember a familiar story about a certain spy who was sent by his commanders to an enemy territory, and he had specific goals to accomplish for his country. However, in order to do that, this spy had to move to this foreign land and actually live within the enemy territory in order for him to eventually be very familiar with the enemy's tradition, culture, and another way of life. The worst thing happened when he ended up liking his new environment. He became too familiar with the enemy's life situation and totally forgot who he truly was and his true nationality and identity. The very life and culture that he was fighting against became who he was in the end. In movies, a spy like him is called to have "gone dark." How many of so-called God's followers today have "gone dark?" They have become too familiar with the ways of this world that you can no longer distinguish them from "real citizens of the world." They have been doing almost everything that this world is doing, and there is no more distinction. They talk like the world; they walk like the world; and they do practically everything that the world does. They have become ineffective in fulfilling the Great Commission because they have lost credibility in showing to others that they are living their lives according to what they preach. In fact, a lot of Christians no longer share the Gospel with anyone because they simply don't have a strong life testimony. Nobody will listen to them because they are just like everyone else.

The enemy, being the prince of lies, will constantly cast doubts in our minds making us feel that after we fall down, after we succumb to his temptations, we are no longer worthy to come back to God. This is one of the lies our enemy has specialized over centuries. He will be the one who lures us into sin and the first one to make us feel unworthy in coming back to God. This is where a lot of people fail by not being able to recognize that the enemy is bound to make their lives miserable, and they forget the promises of the Good Shepherd in His word. After sinking too deep in their sins, they thought that God has forgotten them. They thought that since God is holy, He has no room for allowing His children to commit mistakes and encounter failures. But we should know better than that. God knows that we are not perfect, and while we are still in the flesh, He expects us to commit sins. He does not expect perfection, but He instead expects obedience. Although sin offends our Holy God, He offers second chances. He never gets tired of welcoming us back. All He expects from us is to come to Him with a truly repentant heart. Like a Good Shepherd, we are like those sheep in His flock who go astray. We are always welcome to come back to the flock. If we are genuinely part of His flock, when we sin, He expects us to be convicted by the Holy Spirit, which leads us to ask forgiveness from Him and repent. The Bible tells us in 1 John 1:9, *"If we confess our sins, he is faithful and just and will forgive us our sins and purify us from all unrighteousness."* Remember that once a person is saved, once a person has truly surrendered his or her life to Christ and has accepted Him as Savior and Lord, the enemy cannot do anything to take this salvation away. He is already sealed by the Holy Spirit. Jesus said in John 10:28, *"I give them eternal life, and they shall never perish; no one will snatch them out of my hand."* All the enemy can do is to make our lives miserable while we are here on earth, a life full of guilt and regret after he lured us into sinning and experiencing temporary, skin-deep pleasures.

When King David committed the sin of adultery and murder, he repented. These are terrible sins, but then He asked for forgiveness after realizing his mistakes. At one point, he prayed to God, *"Restore to me the joy of Your salvation"* (Ps. 51:12a). Salvation cannot be lost, but the joy of being saved can. This is the reason why we ask for forgiveness when we sin. We pray for forgiveness not to get saved over and over again. But instead, we pray for forgiveness to ask God to restore the joy of being saved, to restore the relationship we have with Him. If we truly received Jesus Christ in our lives as our Good Shepherd, as our personal Lord and Savior, our salvation is secured; and it lasts for eternity. We shall not make any mistake about this reality. This is a fact, and this is why the enemy is trying to cast doubts into our minds. We must always remember these very important passages from the book of Hebrews, which is a favorite of mine: *"It is impossible for those who have once been enlightened, who have tasted the heavenly gift, who have shared in the Holy Spirit, who have tasted the goodness of the word of God and the powers of the coming age and who have fallen away, to be brought back to repentance. To their loss they are crucifying the Son of God all over again and subjecting him to public disgrace"* (6:4–6). When God says "it's impossible" to lose your salvation, then it simply means it is impossible!

This pretty much reminds me of the relationship of a father to his son. This is one important metaphor that God uses to describe our relationship with Him. We call Him our Father. I am really thankful for being blessed by the Lord to become a father to two wonderful children, my daughter and my son. I usually bring my only son to school in the morning. When he was much younger, every morning that I bring him to school, we always do a "secret handshake" in the car, and we usually do it with a music background. Whatever music that was popular during those days, for as long as the beat will go well with our "secret handshake," we were going to do it. I always tell a joke about it by telling him that I need to confirm every morning that he is indeed my son or he was not abducted by aliens and that he was not an impostor so we need to do that "secret handshake." We enjoyed doing the handshake morning after morning. This is one of my memorable bonding moments with my son. Like any other child, my son sometimes disobeys my wife or me, and we get offended as parents because of his actions, whether intentional or not. Sometimes

I will not talk to him when I'm angry, and obviously, our relationship gets affected. Sometimes when I was angry with him, I will not initiate the "secret handshake" and will just be quiet all the time. But you see, no matter how offended I was, or my wife was, he is still no doubt our son. He still bears my surname, and he is still part of the family. I do not suspend his privilege to use my surname because he committed a sin. He is still my son, and nothing can change that. It is only our relationship that suffers for the moment. When he asks for forgiveness and we reconciled, then our relationship is restored. We'll do the secret handshake again, and we shall once again feel the warmth and intimate fellowship that we used to enjoy. It is very similar to our relationship with God as our Good Shepherd. We are the sheep of His flock; nothing can change that. We belong to His care. It is also similar to our relationship with God as our Abba Father. If we are His child, nothing can change that. We carry His surname. We are called His children, and that will last for eternity.

The Good Shepherd *prepares a table before me in the presence of my enemy.* God knows each and every opposition that we may ever face here in this world. He is not surprised that we end up making enemies because when Jesus walked on earth, He made enemies as well. His enemies caused Him too much trouble. His enemies hurt not only Him but the people He loves. This is the reason why the Good Shepherd can relate to each and every situation we may encounter because He Himself experienced those things.

> **God allows the enemy to engage us in those daily battles because He knows that we need these experiences to grow and mature in our faith spiritually.**

Jesus had been mocked, flogged, and even crucified but in His dying breath, He uttered words of forgiveness for His enemies. He said in Luke 23:34, *"Father, forgive them, for they do not know what they are doing."* Despite all the humiliation and torture that our Lord Jesus Christ received from His enemies, He knew that He can find ultimate comfort and care from God the Father. Many times, Jesus went to a solitary place to find comfort from the Father. Jesus wants to assure us that we can also find ultimate comfort and protection from Him. We do not have to be afraid of our enemy because we have the assurance that Christ already has victory, He has won the war! It is the daily battles with the enemy that we need to face and be victorious of. God allows the enemy to engage us in those daily battles because He knows that we need these experiences to grow and mature in our faith spiritually. The picture of God preparing a table for us in the presence of our enemy shows that He has graciously accepted us into His household where there is ultimate protection from any kind of harm that the enemy will instigate against us in this life. *"Preparing a table"* for us means that we can stand tall, confident, and face our adversaries that we can become victors and not just victims in our daily battles. A lot of people think that they can face their daily battles alone. They thought they will never need any help, and by using their own abilities and skills, they can ward off any kind of obstacle and defeat their enemies. They are wrong. They cannot do it alone. Jesus said we cannot do anything apart from Him, and this includes engaging battle and winning against our enemies. Only God can give us the ultimate victory that we have been longing for in life. How many people are in bondage with so many things today? They just get by but not really achieving victory over their bondage and over their battles. Only by realizing that by being in God's household and protection we can face the enemy head-on. We can win not because of our own abilities but because we are under the great care and protection by the Good Shepherd. We are empowered by Him through the ministry of the Holy Spirit to engage in battle and win.

There are times in our lives when we feel that everyone else around us seem to be against us. How many times do we hear people saying they have nobody in their lives anymore to understand them and everyone seems to be their enemy? This experience can sometimes lead to an even more serious situation like depression and anxiety. Growing up or even when I was in my mid-to-late twenties, I don't remember making a lot of enemies. I

> **A true friend has the audacity to rebuke you and tell you point-blank that you are wrong.**

have made some pretty good accomplishments in my studies and professional career, and it was smooth sailing. In the "secular world," if you work really hard, there is a big chance that you will make it and achieve your dreams. As a person, I can say I am pretty much sociable and friendly, and I can easily make good friends. When I became a pastor of a Christian church, there were times when things turn out a bit different than what I expected. I thought that since in most times I would be dealing with people who are professing to be Christians, life will be simple and my life as a pastor would be a "walk in the park." What can go wrong if you are dealing with people who claim to be followers of Christ? I was wrong. I realized over the years that I have been a pastor that it is even more difficult to handle a church. It is much more complicated to handle matters of relationships especially when emotions are involved. As a pastor, I have personally experienced being questioned of my integrity by people whom I treated as brothers in faith. Sometimes in our passion and desire to fulfill our calling, people get offended. No matter how good our intentions are, when it comes to a matter of rebuke or discipline, people resist and tried to reason out and get offended. It is unfortunate that sometimes some people are on the wrong side of the fence. They treat those who have genuine concern over them as enemies and consider others who just always agree with them as friends. They got it mixed up. A true friend has the audacity to rebuke you and tell you point-blank that you are wrong. Proverbs 17:17 tells us, "*A friend loves at all times, and a brother is born for a time of adversity.*" Sometimes, we hang out with the wrong people. They like to be "friends" with us during good times or during times of plenty. We consider those people as friends because they tell us things that we want to hear. But when problems come, they are the first ones to disappear. The proverb I quoted above tells us that those true friends don't abandon you during the tough times. In fact, this verse tells us that when you experience hard times, you'll know whom among your friends will stand by and be with you throughout your challenge. Jesus had some really good friends while He was here on earth. He's got his twelve disciples who went with Him everywhere he goes. He taught them a lot of things, and they were firsthand witnesses to His miracles. He multiplied bread with them; He walked on water; He healed the sick; He made the blind see; and He raised the dead. They spent a great deal of time together, and He considered them

His friends. Unfortunately, in that company of twelve, He's got one enemy. His name is *Judas Iscariot* who sold Him for thirty pieces of silver. Judas's heart was never right from the start, but Jesus gave Him the opportunity to change His ways. However, Judas's heart was corrupt, and even after being with Jesus for a while, he took advantage of his position in the ministry and in the end. He let the enemy rule over his mind, corrupted his heart, and he ended up betraying Christ.

The Bible has a lot to say about our enemy, the devil. Even before the creation of this world, this enemy has been opposing God, and since he knows that he cannot hurt God, he tries to destroy His creation. He tries to get back at Him by attacking the apple of His eyes. He will always attempt to make our lives miserable. The more we get involved in God's work, the more this enemy will try to hurt us and make us feel defeated. But he is the one who is actually beaten, and he knows that. Jesus has achieved ultimate victory over the enemy in the cross. The devil knows that at the end of days, he will forever be punished in the lake of fire. In the meantime, he tries to steal our joy and make us feel worthless. This is the best that he can do. This is the *only* thing he can do. We always hear the saying, "The war has been won, it is the small battles that you have to deal with." If you are a child of God, your salvation is secured, and the enemy cannot do anything to change that. God has already won the war. We just need to be victorious in our daily battles in life. The Apostle John assures us in 1 John 4:4 that *"you, dear children, are from God and have overcome them, because the one who is in you is greater than the one who is in the world."* He is speaking here of Jesus Christ, and if we have Christ in our lives, we are greater than the enemy. He cannot do any permanent harm on us. He cannot do anything to hurt us that God will not allow. We must always remember that as we struggle in our lives here on earth, the battle is always spiritual. Our enemy is not that mean person in the office; it's not that mean kid at school; it's not even our spouse or our in-laws; and it's not that mean neighbor either. Our enemy is the devil, and the battle we fight is spiritual. The Apostle Paul warns us in Ephesians 6:12, *"For our struggle is not against flesh and blood, but against the rulers, against the authorities, against the powers of this dark world and against the spiritual forces of evil in the heavenly realms."* This is an important reality that each one of us must be very aware of. We fight daily spiritual battles. Most of our other issues that have physical repercussions are usually a result of spiritual battles.

Loving someone who is lovable is probably the easiest thing to do. In fact, nobody needs to tell us to love those who love us. It is easy for us to love those people who are close to us. This is the reason why they are called "loved ones." Jesus has something to say to us in regard to how we shall treat our enemies, and this is mind-blowing. He commands us to love our enemies! He said in Matthew 5:44, *"But I tell you, love your enemies and pray for those who persecute you."* This command probably defies all reason and logic. The world will laugh at us when they learned that God expects us not only to pray for our enemies and how can they understand that we are to love our enemies as well. Some people asked me before if they can pray for their enemies, that their house gets burned or they get sick or they go bankrupt. This is not the kind of prayer that God expects us to do for our enemies. God knows that it is in our nature to try and get even, but we must understand that when the Good Shepherd commands us to love our enemies and pray for those who persecute us, it doesn't mean that those people who offended us or have done us wrong can go scot-free and that they won't be accountable anymore to what they have done. It simply means that when we love our enemies and pray for those who persecute us, we are letting God act on our behalf, and we are lifting our burdens to Him. When we have this attitude of loving our enemies and praying for those who persecute us, God is changing us from the inside out. He is making our faith in Him grow, and He is making us humble. I believe one reason why Jesus wants us to love our enemies is that He knows that those we consider enemies here in this world are not our real enemies. They are being used by the real enemies to hurt us and make our lives difficult. For sure they will be accountable to God for every hurt they have caused us and every misery they brought into our lives, but we should let God be God and let Him vindicate us.

According to Pastor Rick Warren in his book *Purpose Driven Life*, *"True humility is not thinking less of yourself but thinking of your-*

self less." In these times we live in, the world tells us always to get even, to fight back, not to be an underdog or not to be a pushover.

> God gives "out of this world" commands, and most of the time they don't make sense simply because we are not of this world.

This world is teaching us to be strong, but usually, the strength that is not anchored on the Lord is only a superficial strength. It is skin deep, and it is only strength on the outside. Deep inside, a lot of people feel so weak and defeated. God did not say we become like doormats, and people will just keep on stepping on us. God wants us to trust Him that He can fairly and justly act on our behalf. Loving your enemies and praying for those who persecute you is a totally "out of this world" command, but it still makes sense. Do you know why? God gives "out of this world" commands, and most of the time they don't make sense simply because we are not of this world. A lot of God commands will always be seen as out of this world because God sees things outside of this world, He sees beyond reason or logic, and we cannot always rationalize His thoughts and actions because we are not God. He is way above our heads! He sees things from an eternal or heavenly perspective, and so must we. If we don't try to see things from His heavenly and eternal perspective and we just keep on looking at things from a worldly or temporal perspective, we can never understand commands like *"loving your enemies and praying for those who persecute you."* Jesus commands us in Luke 6:29, *"If someone slaps you on one cheek, turn to them the other also. If someone takes your coat, do not withhold your shirt from them."* These are out-of-this-world commands for sure, but I hope and pray because of these explanations we would understand better why God expects us to be different from the rest.

When Jesus walked on earth, He defied not just tradition but logic as well. The Jews thought He was crazy, and the Pharisees believed He was up for something. I can imagine how Jesus's listeners reacted when He told them to love their enemies. It is easy to love somebody who is loveable like our spouse, children, parents, relatives, friends, or even our dogs. But it takes too much courage to love someone who has offended us. It is equally difficult, if not impossible, to pray for them. Jesus did not say that as we love and pray for our enemies, we need to trust them again. Of course not! Trust takes

> **It is easy to love somebody who is loveable like our spouse, children, parents, relatives, friends, or even our dogs. But it takes too much courage to love someone who has offended us.**

time. Trust needs to be earned again. If there is somebody who wronged us, it will take a while for us to give them our trust again.

I was watching a really disturbing news one day about a grandfather who has abused his own granddaughter who was entrusted to him by the parents who went out of town. He was caught by the police and was put in jail. When the mother of the girl was interviewed if she can ever forgive her own father for what he has done, she said maybe she can because that is God's command. But trusting this person again is another thing. She said it will take a long time before she can ever let any of her kids go near to this man again. God knows that reconciliation takes the participation of both parties. Both must be willing to be reconciled. God's command to forgive somebody like this man for his wrongdoings, heinous as it

> **Forgiveness must not rely solely on our emotions but based on a heart obedient to the Good Shepherd's command.**

may, does not mean he can be free from the consequences of his sins. No. He will have to face those consequences and God, who is just and fair, will definitely deal with him in His own terms and in His own time.

God's command to those people whom this man has wronged was actually for the benefit of the victims so they can be free from that bondage inside their hearts, they can lift everything to God and move on with their lives. We have to forgive immediately since it is God's command, no matter how bad we feel about the situation. Forgiveness must not rely solely on our emotions but based on a heart obedient to the Good Shepherd's command. Jesus will never ask us to do something that He can never do. While hanging on the cross, one of the final words He uttered was a prayer of forgiveness for those who wronged Him. We don't have to carry an unforgiving heart to our deathbed. A lot of people find it hard to live better lives with their hearts filled with anger and hate because they are not willing to let go and forgive. They have made it their life's mission always to remember the hurt caused to them by other people. In the end, they do not realize it, but they have more to lose by being a bitter person, and their lives become miserable.

Being part of God's flock, we must be thankful that our Good Shepherd is always there to protect us from our enemies. A lot of times, we feel alone in our battles. A lot of times, we think that nobody is taking our sides, and it seems that everyone we know is against us. We must realize that for as long that our hearts are truthful and we are confident that we bring glory to God in everything we do, we must not be afraid of anything even if everyone seems to turn their backs against us. We must not be worried that we will be left alone in our own battles. We are never alone. The Good Shepherd is there to fight our battles for us. All we need to do is to trust Him well enough and lift up everything to Him. Sometimes we get tired of our daily battles because we are fighting the wrong ones. A lot of these battles are not our own battles. We must be smart enough to know which ones are ours and which ones are not. We must learn to pick our battles. We already learned earlier that the battle we fight against are actually spiritual battles. Especially in a husband-and-wife relationship, we must recognize that our enemy, the devil, will try everything he could in his power to destroy marriage and make our families miserable. If we think our enemy is our spouse or our mean boss at work or the unfair teacher in school or the corrupt politician in the government, we are mistaken because our real enemy is the devil. If we recognize that our battle with the true enemy is spiritual, then we must retaliate with something spiritual as well. In Ephesians 6:17, God wants us to *"take the helmet of salvation and the sword of the Spirit, which is the word of God."* Our best weapon against the enemy is the Word of God. Much can be learned from our Good Shepherd Himself when He had a face-off with His enemy in the wilderness. After fasting forty days and forty nights, Jesus was hungry. Matthew 4:3 tells us, *"The tempter came to him and said, 'If you are the Son of God, tell these stones to become bread.'"* We must be aware that during those times that we feel we have accomplished something significant especially in the ministry or in our spiritual life, like in this case, Jesus just finished fasting, the enemy can always come during a time when we least expect it to ruin our success and tempt us. What's interesting here was the reply of Jesus. In Matthew 4:4, *"Jesus answered, 'It is written: Man shall not live on bread alone, but on every word that comes from the mouth of God.'"* Jesus answered His enemy's temptation by using the Word of God. He quoted the Old Testament, specifically Deuteronomy 8:3. Another valuable lesson to learn here about our Good Shepherd is that He will always be there to protect us. He will send his angels to comfort us and make us victorious in our daily battles. This is what God did for His Son, and this is certainly what God will do for His children as well.

Have you ever crossed behind the enemy's lines? Sometimes we get into trouble because we are treading on dangerous places. It's hard for us to remain victorious in our daily battles if the company or people we spend our time with are the representatives or agents of our enemy. We must stay with the flock so we can be protected and not be left alone in the enemy's territory. We must always recognize and be aware if we are crossing the enemy's line already and our flock can help remind us of those things. We cannot stay behind the enemy's line and not expect to get hurt. We must learn how to operate within our own boundaries.

It reminds me a story that I heard from many preachers and read in history books about the German battleship *Bismarck* in the spring of 1940 when the war was starting to wage between England and Germany. The *Bismarck* was the most massive and most powerful battleship at that time, and it had the reputation of being unsinkable as its armor was very thick that no British torpedo can fire through it. In one encounter with the British navy, a torpedo hit the Bismarck in its rudder causing the huge fleet to be able to maneuver in circles, and it ended up behind enemy lines. In May of 1940, the British navy finally sunk the unsinkable battleship. Sometimes we think that our enemies are unsinkable and formidable, but if we are able to attack it with the right weapon, our enemies will just go on circles. For a Christian, our rudder is the Word of God. It guides us in the right direction and prevents us from ending up behind enemy lines.

The Good Shepherd must be the one to pilot our lives. We must yield to His lordship and obey His directions.

Reflection Questions

1. Did you have enemies while you were growing up?
2. How does it feel knowing that somebody does not like you?
3. How does it feel knowing that there is someone whom you can go to for comfort and protection against the works of your enemy?

God's Anointing and Our Overflowing Cup

You anoint my head with oil, my cup overflows.
—Psalm 23:5b

Anointing oil is mentioned more than fifteen times in the Scripture. In the Old Testament, oil was used for pouring on the head of the high priest. Oil was also being sprinkled at the tabernacle and its furnishings, which symbolizes its holiness and the place is set apart for the Lord. Several times in the Scripture, oil is called anointing oil. The Jews were not allowed to reproduce the anointing oil for personal use. It's not something they can just get from anywhere. The oil was usually composed of myrrh, cinnamon, and other ingredients. The preparation of anointing oil was an elaborate process as it requires strict compliance to minute details in terms of ingredients and process. Its mere preparation tests the obedience of the Israelites, and it symbolizes and even demonstrates the holiness of God. I remember when God gave instructions to Noah to build the ark, it contains precise measurements and dimensions. While it represents God's perfection and His attention to details, I believe it is also a test of Noah's obedience and patience. God probably wants to test him if he was paying attention to each and every word that He was telling Him. He wanted to give Noah a chance to show his obedience by following His instructions word for word and down to the last measurement. Sometimes God requires us to do things the long and tedious way or even the hard way, and oftentimes we question God why. Why can't we just take the easy route? Why can't we just take the shortcut if we'll produce the same results anyway? We cannot always understand why He would want us to go through something so elaborate or something so detailed when in fact, in our own wisdom and understanding, we can do it in a much shorter and simpler way. The answer is maybe because God wants to test our patience and obedience. He wants to see if we are paying attention. It is in small details that we sometimes learn important lessons in life and not necessarily in bigger things. We just need to pay attention. It is easy to miss important details when things or events that are happening in our lives are big and great. But if we sit down and start pondering upon God's little instructions, this is the time we learn some of life's lessons. It reminds me of a story in the Old Testament more than three thousand years ago when the Israelites were in the desert.

The Lord delivered the Israelites from their bondage in Egypt, and after crossing the Red Sea, they were to take possession of the land God had promised their forefathers. The promised land was described as a land *"flowing with milk and honey"* (Exod. 3:8). However, the Israelites were not confident that they can drive the current inhabitants from the land. They were afraid, and they did not trust God well enough that He who delivered them out of Egypt can undoubtedly help them oust those occupants even if they look giants from their sight. The Israelites' unbelief and lack of trust in God resulted in God cursing them with forty years of wandering in the wilderness until all the unbelieving generation passed away. For those who marched out of Egypt through the parted Red Sea, they were never able to step foot on the promised land except for the two faithful spies, Joshua and Caleb, who believed that God can certainly help them conquer the promised land. These two spies saw the greatness of God rather than the bigness of their problems. Historians say that crossing the desert could have only taken the Israelites approximately eleven days, but God did not allow them to cross over because of their unbelief. The Israelites who crossed from Egypt were anointed by God to conquer the promised land, but because of their attitudes, the fulfillment of their destiny only happened in the next generation. It's so unfortunate that those Israelites who witnessed all the miracles performed by God in Egypt and even after they miraculously crossed the Red Sea seemed to be not enough to give them the confidence to conquer the promised land. Maybe some people will ask why did God require the Israelites to conquer the land? Can't He just hand over those lands on a silver platter? He is God, and I believe that God can surely do that. If He desires, He can just let the Israelites march through those lands where no blood will be shed and no waiting necessary. But I have always believed that sometimes, God will not do by miracle what He wants us to do out of obedience. There are important lessons to be learned whenever He wants us to do things the hard way. Sadly, those Israelites missed the blessing from God that would have resulted from their obedience to God's command.

Are you being instructed by God to obey His specific commands? Are you patient enough to concentrate on the details? God does not want you to miss the important lessons that He has prepared as you go through those periods of waiting or periods of preparation working on the details. It is in those meticulous and detailed instructions that God molds us into something better. He wants us to learn to be patient and build our character that is why He expects us to obey and follow Him to the letter.

In the New Testament, several passages refer to the practice of anointing with oil, and we can conclude from those passages how the anointing of oil was being used or being referred to. Mark 6:13 tells us that *"they drove out many demons and anointed many sick people with oil and healed them."* Same holds true in James 5:14, which says, *"Is anyone among you sick? Let them call the elders of the church to pray over them and anoint them with oil in the name of the Lord."* In both instances, anointing of oil was used for healing. It should be noted that the anointing oil in itself has no power to heal the sickness of any person, but it is the power of the One whom the oil represents. The oil represents the Holy Spirit. Every child of God is anointed by Him with the Holy Spirit indwelling in his life. Being anointed means being set apart by God for a special calling. The oil, in this case, symbolizes the Holy Spirit who alone can empower us to fulfill God's calling in our lives. Without Him (the Holy Spirit) there is no way we can accomplish such a calling. Without the ministry of the Holy Spirit, there is no way we can glorify God. Simply stated, in our time today and looking at it from a spiritual perspective, anointing symbolizes our being empowered by God through the Holy Spirit. Our true anointing comes from our Lord Himself, our Good Shepherd. We should not get caught in that danger of idolatry where we think that the oil itself is the source of power as it will turn our focus away from the true Source of power. A lot of people fell into this trap. Some even did lots of businesses out of it. You can see merchandisers outside those big churches selling different kinds of oil with the claim that those oils can heal and make people well. While in some cases, these oils have medicinal components, so there is also some sort of scientific explanation why the oil heals, but the ultimate source of healing is still our Good Shepherd who alone can anoint us with spiritual oil and provide ultimate healing, both physically and—most especially—spiritually. Didn't God heal us from being sick and infected by sin?

Anointing oil also represents worship. The Gospel of Mark in 14:3–9 tells us that Mary anointed Jesus's feet with an expensive alabaster flask of oil made of pure nard, and she did this as an act of worship. This story tells us that God deserves the highest form of worship from His children. In John 12:5, one of Jesus's disciples

> Our anointing comes with a very expensive price; Jesus had to die on the cross to save us.

even questioned Mary's act of worship. He said, *"Why wasn't this perfume sold and the money given to the poor? It was worth a year's wages."* What a "noble" statement, and at the onset, I see nothing wrong with it. But we know that this disciple was Judas Iscariot who later on betrayed Jesus. We also know that Judas was not sincere when he said this. He was mismanaging their funds, and he was probably thinking that if Mary just sold this perfume and gave the proceeds to their funds, then maybe Judas will unjustly benefit from it. This anointing oil, which was poured by Mary on Jesus's feet and wiped His feet with her hair, was a very costly perfume. The Bible says that it was made from pure nard, and it was so expensive that it was equivalent to one year's wage of typical laborers at that time. When God anoints us with the Holy Spirit, it's not cheap. Our anointing comes with a very expensive price; Jesus had to die on the cross to save us. The moment we respond to His invitation, we are anointed by the Holy Spirit. For this reason alone, God is worthy of our worship.

There is another significance of *"anointing of oil"* in history especially during biblical times, and this is from a more practical standpoint. This is not necessarily something spiritual or even ritual-istic. In the Middle East, especially during biblical era, people usually travel on foot or ride on animals such as camels, horses, or donkeys in the desert—which was typically hot, dry, and sometimes humid. This is one reason why they cover their head from the rays of the sun as the sunrays can cause their head to become so dry that it feels like it can almost crack the skull because of the scorching heat. We should also remember from the Old Testament, for about forty years, the Israelites were wandering in the desert. They were living in tempo-rary dwellings like tents, and even though crossing to the promised land could have only taken them a few days, they kept moving only whenever they receive specific instruction from God. It took them forty years to finally cross over to the promised land because they can only move whenever God told them to. God's *pillar of cloud* covered the tabernacle, and whenever this cloud lifted from the tabernacle, that's the only time the people of Israel can move and set out on their journey. If the cloud did not rise, they remained where they were and wait for the Lord's next instructions as to when it will be lifted again so they can continue on with their journey. The cloud of the Lord hovered over the tabernacle during the day, and it looked like a *pillar of fire* at night so the whole Israel could see it even from afar.

Even during King David's time, there were still a lot of wan-derers in the desert. People have traveled through miles and miles of dry land just to go from one destination to another. Because of this long travels, people have to stop over at various places to rest, refresh, and regain their strength. A lot of times, they were being received by gracious hosts whom they would encounter along their way. It was customary for these hosts to receive them and anoint or pour down oil to their visitors. Usually, they will pour oil over the visitor's head and let it flow. This was more of a traditional, hospitable, and gracious gesture. What a relief the anointing oil provides under these circumstances! It provides the much-needed moisture to the head and allows the traveler to be refreshed, regain his strength, and be ready to continue on with his journey. Imagine if you are the person who traveled hundreds of miles in the desert and you end up visiting the tent of a very gracious host who anoints your head with oil. What a relief! What a tremendous source of comfort! It keeps your head hydrated, and it keeps you calm and relaxes your nerves.

In modern times, we use the word *anointing* to mean God's unique calling for someone to serve Him in the church ministry. We sometimes hear this word whenever we pray for pastors and church leaders, for God's anointing be upon them. A popular maxim that you have probably heard goes like this: "When God appoints, He anoints and He does not disappoint!" I believe that anointing usually comes first before appointing. God's appointment only confirms that we have been anointed earlier, especially with the spiritual gifts that God has given us to perform and accomplish the "appointing." King David finally got his appointment to sit on the throne of Israel approximately fifteen years after he was first anointed by God through the prophet Samuel.

I believe having experienced a similar kind of anointing with regard to my calling as a preacher. My first experience to deliver a sermon happened on a Good Friday, and if my memory serves me right, in the year 2002. I was assigned to deliver a five-minute sermon at our church's Seven Last Words service. There were six other preachers, and our assignment was to exhort on the seven last words of Jesus Christ on the cross. It was my first time speaking to a congregation of thousands, and I remember I was so tensed that I needed to even check-in to a hotel nearby the night before as I didn't want to be late, and I wanted to be comfortable. My wife even invited her whole family so we can also minister to them through that Good Friday service. I remember the scripture that I exhorted was found in Matthew 27:46, *"About three in the afternoon Jesus cried out in a loud voice, "Eli, Eli, lema sabachthani?"* (which means, *"My God, my God, why have you forsaken me?")* I was the fourth speaker out of seven, which made me exactly the middle one. After my turn and as I walked down the stage, a visiting pastor from Australia hugged me so tight and whispered in my ear, "*Brother, you have the anointing. You have a gift, I hope and pray you will nurture that gift.*" At that time, I didn't realize what he was talking about. I was definitely not in my right head after that sermon. To me, it was just a five-minute sermon, and I didn't even have a way of knowing how it has impacted the congregation except of course from the clapping of their hands, which I can barely hear because of my shock and awe. I was even more pressured because my wife's whole family was there. Sadly, it took me another seven years before stepping on the podium once again and deliver God's word to our church here in Vancouver, British Columbia. I didn't take heed of that pastor's advice to nurture the gift that God has given me, but sadly, I moved on with my life and went on to do other things. In retrospect, I now believe that my *anointing* to become a preacher has started way back then. I firmly believe that this pastor was used by God to communicate His message for me that I have the anointing. But God has withheld my *appointing* for the next seven years maybe because I wasn't ready and maybe because He wanted me to experience more in life, which I can use to be a more effective messenger of His word. I thank God that He still gave me the opportunity to respond to my calling and fulfill my anointing. God certainly did not give up on me.

Maybe God has given your anointing already, but either you are not submitting to His will as you still want to prioritize other things in your life, or you are just trying to run away from Him maybe because you feel inadequate or unworthy of your anointing. Either way, you are missing a excellent opportunity to serve the Lord in an area where He specifically called you to serve Him.

Finally, the writer of Hebrews used a very important metaphor concerning anointing oil. He wrote in Hebrews 1:8–9, "*But about the Son, he says, "Your throne, O God, will last forever and ever; a scepter of justice will be the scepter of your kingdom. You have loved righteousness and hated wickedness; therefore God, your God, has set you above your companions by anointing you with the oil of joy.*" This is what God the Father was telling to His Begotten Son Jesus Christ as He returns triumphantly to heaven. I believe these passages tell us the ultimate representation and symbolism of anointing oil as coming from God the Father Himself in reference to His Son. It also affirms and strengthens the doctrine of Trinity in a sense that God the Father addresses the Son as *"O God."* It is therefore very important to note that the use of anointing oil even for symbolism must not be taken lightly as it represents no less than God the Father glorifying the Son by anointing Him with the oil of joy.

Aside from the anointing of oil, the fifth verse also talks about how the guest's "cup overflows," which is a good example of the host's generosity. Pouring wine or anything to drink on someone's cup up to the point of overflowing represents generosity, hospitality, and even abundance. In modern times, it is more of a welcome drink or sometimes even a toast being offered during special occasions. In the Middle East, pouring drink is a significant gesture from a host when receiving his guest as it was always assumed that the guest comes from a very warm, humid, and even tiring journey.

I had the opportunity to visit a place in China called Fuzhou City in the province of Fujian. I learned later that this city was one of the most important Protestant mission fields in China. No wonder I have noticed quite a number of Christian churches in the area. In some of the dinners I had been to in this city, I realized that offering a drinking toast was very customary. As we were having dinner in a big round table, the host would go around and propose a toast in honor of each of his guest. You can have whatever drink you are comfortable with, like wine or fruit juice, but it was the gesture of being received and honored by your host that is more important. If you try to drink wine during these toasts, I can guarantee you that you will be very drunk after dinner because the toast is made several times by the host and by each member of his family.

One trait that Filipinos can be very proud of and is known throughout the world is their characteristic of being hospitable. Filipinos love to welcome and entertain guests. These can be their relatives, friends, important people in the community, or even total strangers. During special occasions like town fiestas, birthday celebrations, wedding receptions, or even Christmas dinners, they serve all kinds of food and drinks, and it is indeed overflowing. I remember whenever we visit my wife's family and relatives during special occasions, she has an aunt there who was usually in-charge of preparing and cooking the food. After she gives me an empty plate, she will make it a point that I get everything. She will put food on my plate, and the more I say no, the more she gets excited to put even more. I knew she will be offended if I didn't try all the dishes that she has prepared, so I would end up really stuffed and bloated after having dinner at their place. During special occasions and whenever Filipinos have visitors, they will serve you their best dishes. They will use their best silver utensils, those that they only use during special occasions. The expensive plates will have to be removed from the cupboard and used only for those times that they have visitors. They don't use these utensils in their daily meals. These utensils are reserved, again for special occasions. A lot of times these utensils are dusty, but the gracious host will make sure to clean them thoroughly and have them used by the special visitors during these special occasions. They will make sure the tablecloths are either new or fresh from the laundry. Whenever they pour wine or soft drinks on your glass, it will overflow. Whenever they add dishes to your plate, it will definitely overflow on your plate like a huge pile of food. And when the guests are about to go home, they will definitely have some food to bring back to for their family whom they left at home. Filipino hosts will have special plastic boxes or bags prepared and "ready to go" so that when the guests are about to leave, they have some food to bring home. This is how a gracious host treats his guest. The way the gracious host treats his guest reflects a lot about his or her own personality. The host obviously does not want to ruin his or her own reputation by not treating the guests properly. The host does not want the people in their town to talk about their family not being a gracious host to their visitors. This is very much against the culture in the Philippines, especially in small towns.

The Bible also tells us that we should do good things to people, especially to fellow believers in the Lord. The Apostle Paul tells us in Galatians 6:10, *"Therefore, as we have opportunity, let us do good to all people, especially to those who belong to the family of believers."* This is consistent with the famous adage, "Charity begins at home." In a church setting, we are very familiar with holding our home group fellowships and Bible studies in different homes. A homegroup is an essential extension of the church. As more and more people become part of a particular congregation, it is very important to be involved in small Bible study groups. As each family receives its small groups for Bible studies in their homes, it becomes an excellent venue and opportunity to show hospitality and kindness toward the other members of the group especially when there is a new attendee. Our own homes are blessings from God. He owns it, and we are just stewards of God's properties; and if we are able to use these homes to welcome others, make them feel at home and be gracious to them, God is pleased, and we become good and faithful caretakers of His blessings.

Our life with the Good Shepherd is similar to how a gracious host treats his guests regarding the overflowing cup and the anointing of oil. God certainly anoints us with oil, which symbolizes not only the ultimate comfort and healing that only He can provide, but it also represents our important calling in life coming from Him. The Good Shepherd also "overflows our cups" to make sure that we are equipped

> **The Good Shepherd also "overflows our cups" to make sure that we are equipped with the necessary skills and gifts in order for us to respond and fulfill His calling.**

with the necessary skills and gifts for us to respond and fulfill His calling. God overflows our cup as He provides to a lot of people not only the things that they need but also the things that they want. Overflowing our cup also represents all those blessings that our Good Shepherd provides. How many of us would complain to God sometimes when we are not able to buy what we need to buy or get what we need to get? God is not obligated to give us anything, but because of His generosity and compassion, He allows us to get the things that we don't necessarily need. God is not stingy. He pours out excessive love and blessing to those who love Him. If you look at your lives today, I don't think what you have or possess are only those things that you really need. I am sure there are so many things that we possess in our lives today are not really necessary. These are things that we only want, and yet, our Good Shepherd graciously allows us to own these things. In fact, if you look at your stockroom, there are so many things there that you want to dispose of during springtime or make a garage sale so we can get rid of those items. It is amazing that the Holy Spirit is not only represented by the anointing of oil but by the overflowing cup as well. In one verse, King David makes a wonderful application of the Holy Spirit in the life of a believer. If we surrender our lives to the Good Shepherd, He overflows our lives with the Holy Spirit.

The Apostle Paul wrote in Ephesians 5:18, *"Do not get drunk on wine, which leads to debauchery. Instead, be filled with the Spirit."* God wants us to have a Spirit-filled life, and He overflows our cup with the infilling of the Holy Spirit in our lives. Jesus promised that if we follow Him and surrender our lives to Him, the Holy Spirit will indwell in us, and this indwelling is permanent. The Holy Spirit is a gift for all believers in Jesus the moment we accept Jesus in our lives (i.e. at the moment of salvation). We are sealed by the Holy Spirit, and He shall indwell in us permanently. "Being filled" with the Spirit is another thing. We won't experience the fullness of the Spirit if we allow sin to overcome us. To be "filled with the Holy Spirit" means that we completely yield to Him to guide us and to control our lives. Being "filled with the Spirit" means we don't grieve Him, and we don't quench His work in us. Being "filled with the Spirit means" we allow Him to be our pilot or captain, and He steers us in the direction where He wants our lives to go. Only by living a life that is obedient to the Good Shepherd are we going to fully manifest the Fruit of the Spirit mentioned by the Apostle Paul to the Galatians 5:22–23, which states, *"But the fruit of the Spirit is love, joy, peace, forbearance, kindness, goodness, faithfulness, gentleness and self-control. Against such things there is no law."*

I believe the Good Shepherd blesses us abundantly, and more than what we need for a very good reason other than for our own benefit. He blesses us so much, more than what we need because He wants us to bless and help others. We are like faucets that should keep on releasing water. A water system that keeps on flowing and releasing water always have clean and fresh water available. If we become stagnant and we stop blessing others, we become like dirty water, unfit for drinking. The things that we get in life are not just for ourselves; it is also intended for other people. We are only channels of God's blessings. If we hold on tight to these things that God has given us to the point that we are becoming self-centered or even selfish, we are technically depriving others of the blessings that they would have received from God through us. These other people would have recognized and known that God cares and provides for them through us. It is a similar thing with our gifts and talents. Our gifts and talents are not given to us by God for our own consumption or enjoyment only. He gave us these gifts so we can bless others. By not using these gifts for example in the ministry, again we are technically depriving others of the blessing that they are supposed to receive. One of the most important character trait that we should develop especially when it comes to responding to our calling is humility. We should not feel that the ministry needs us because of our gifts and talents. Instead, the right attitude is that God gives us the privilege and opportunity to share our gifts and talents to a lot of people especially in the church. If we join any ministry for the wrong reasons, we are bound to fail. If pride gets in the way, we can never be effective in whatever we do for the Lord. The Bible gives us two of the many references about pride: Proverbs 16:18 says, *"Pride goes before destruction, a haughty spirit before a fall"* and James 4:6 *"God opposes the proud but shows favor to the humble."*

King David never lets pride enter his head, and most especially his heart, after he was anointed by the Lord. It took him more than fifteen years to wait for the time he sat down as king of Israel. During those long years, he had several opportunities to kill his opponent Saul, but he chose not to. He did not say, "Well, I was anointed, so let me just take matters into my own hand, and I can take over my throne." King David knew that God's timing is perfect. Sometimes we tend to is to rush on things that we want to do. I believe one of the words synonymous with *anointing* is *waiting*. What are we specifically waiting for after our anointing? We are waiting for God's appointing and a similar case happened to King David. As I study his life, I learned that King David spent a great deal of his life waiting for God's perfect timing in order for him to take the throne.

From the time of God's anointing upon him through the prophet Samuel, he had to wait for at least fifteen years until he became king over Judah, not even the whole of Israel. It takes another seven years before he reigned in the whole of Israel. David's life is a good example of "waiting on the Lord." Not too many of us are very good at waiting. I have mentioned a couple of times while delivering sermons about the importance and the blessing of being patient. The best example of being a patient is how we wait for our turn when seeing a doctor. Have you ever wondered why we are called patients? This is because we have to be really patient in waiting for our turn to be seen by the doctors, especially here in North America (I'm kidding, of course). Sometimes it will take hours before a doctor can actually see us. Sometimes, after lining up for hours, we can even get bumped off especially if there is a more serious case compared to ours. I remember when we were new in Vancouver and our youngest child got sick, we had to bring him to the emergency room of the children's hospital. We had to wait for almost the whole evening. It's terrible, and we were so frustrated. But every time we got bumped off in line, I remember telling my wife that we were still in a better situation because that only means we were not in a life-or-death situation. But the point I am trying to drive here is that sometimes we really have to wait for something that we really want to do or achieve. We have to spend time, and we have to wait for God's perfect timing.

When I decided to take up my master's program in theology, I started by taking up one course at a time without really expecting that one day I will be able to finish a degree. All I was thinking was that I will finish any course that will be a big help in the ministry that I have been called to serve. So I patiently took one class at a time, and after a year and a half, I realized that I already finished half of the program. That was when it dawned on me that there was a possibility that I can complete the program and get the degree by just taking one course at a time so might as well go through all of it. It takes a lot of patience and hard work especially for somebody like me who is a bi-vocational minister, working full-time as a finance executive in another company and, of course, as a full-time pastor, not to mention I have a family to look after. God specializes in being patient.

The Bible tells us a lot about God being patient, and every time I talk about the patience of God, I can think of two very important events and both pertain to the coming of Jesus Christ. First, God is patient enough to wait for His own perfect timing when to send His only begotten Son to be born in this world. Galatians 4:4 tells us *"But when the set time had fully come, God sent his Son, born of a woman, born under the law."* God could have sent the Messiah immediately after the fall of man or during the confusion in the Tower of Babel. Christ could have come after the kingdom of Israel was divided or when the Israelites were enslaved by the Babylonians, but He did not. God waited for His own perfect timing to send Jesus. Imagine the Jews have waited for the Messiah all their lives, but it's ironic that when He came and walked in their midst, they did not recognize Him, and even until now, most of the Jews are still waiting. The Bible says in John 1:11, *"He came to that which was His own, but his own did not receive Him."* For most of us, we can never fully understand God's perfect timing. We just have to trust Him that He is in full control. Second, God is patient enough to *not* yet send Jesus Christ back here on Earth for His second coming. Imagine if Jesus comes back today, a lot of people will perish as they will not have the time to repent of their sins. The Bible tells us in 2 Peter 3:9, *"The Lord is not slow in keeping his promise, as some understand slowness. Instead he is patient with you, not wanting anyone to perish, but everyone to come to repentance."* Jesus said in Matthew 24:14, *"And this gospel of the kingdom will be preached in the whole world as a testimony to all nations, and then the end will come."* I know a lot of people today, believers and followers of Jesus Christ, who have been suffering one way or another, and they want Jesus to finally return. But we must be thankful that He hasn't come back because He knew that we still have a lot to do in terms of sharing His good news to those who need it. Most people are not good with waiting or being patient. As I have mentioned earlier, we live in a world where almost everything is instant. Every information we need is available at our fingertips—the Internet. Our environment today is very much different from how it was thirty years ago.

When I was in college, in order to complete a term paper, we had to go to the library to do our research. We borrowed some books, copied the relevant chapters, go to a business center, rent a typewriter, and then patiently typed our report. It's even harder when you make mistakes. We used what we called a white-out correction fluid. You have to erase one letter at a time and type over it. Nowadays, we use the computer. We don't have to print anything until after we are completely satisfied with our soft copies with the help whatever word-processing software we are using. It is harder to be patient in this world we live in nowadays. But there is still a discipline being built in being patient, most especially when we are trying to understand the will of God regarding our calling in life or even in terms of answers to our prayers. A lot of times, we just don't realize it, but we really have to thank God that He did not answer all our prayers the way we wanted them to be answered. It will be disastrous for us if God will just say yes to everything. God is not a vending machine that we just slide a coin and get whatever we want. God is the source of infinite wisdom. He knows what is best for us. Psalm 130:5–6 tells us, *"I wait for the Lord, my whole being waits, and in his word I put my hope. I wait for the Lord more than watchmen wait for the morning, more than watchmen wait for the morning."* Sometimes God uses the period of waiting to equip us of everything that we need once we get His appointing. I believe King David has learned his best lessons in life while running away from Saul and while waiting for God's perfect timing to make him king over Israel. We just have to be sure that we use these times of waiting and make them times of refreshing to get closer to God and be intimate with Him. This way God will reveal to us the things that we need to do and the character that we need to

> We just have to be sure that we use these times of waiting and make them times of refreshing to get closer to God and be intimate with Him.

> Those unfortunate circumstances in our lives didn't happen for no reason. God, in his almighty power and ultimate wisdom, allows us to experience things in life that we can use to minister to others who are in need.

develop to be more effective in our calling in life. I always hear a common illustration of this about to the relationship of a father to his son. If my son, for example, asks for a car today, even if I am able to buy one for him (although I am not), I will not buy him a car. This is because he is still a teenager, and with the wisdom that I have as his father, I know that it is not good for him to have a car today. And it's illegal, of course! But if my son asks for a car after graduating from university and probably when he is about to start working, and if I am able, there is a big possibility that I will give him what he asks for. Of course, as a father, I will also have to look at his character. Is he the type of person who can be responsible enough to drive a car? Our relationship with God is like that. When God says no to our prayers now, it does not mean that He doesn't want us to get what we want or it doesn't mean He is not able to provide. Sometimes, it only means that we are not ready and He wants us to patiently wait for that time that we can be ready. God knows that He has to say no for the time being. From our perspective, it seems that it is an unanswered prayer, but actually, God answers our prayers; but sometimes, His answer is not always yes, but instead, it's a "no" or "not yet" or "here is something better." So we have to thank God for unanswered prayers, and what we need to do is to keep praying and be intimate with Him. Pray that we understand His will why He is not answering our prayers the way we want it answered.

As I was reflecting on what to write in this book, it gives me the privilege of reflecting on my life as well. At this stage in my life now, I sometimes ask the question, "Am I able to respond and fulfil God's anointing?" I always think that there are still so many things for me to do, but God is not about quantity. He's all for quality. He wants to see us grow in whatever involvement we have when serving Him, wherever we are. He wants to see us disciple others, those who come after us so they too can become effective ministers of the Lord. I hope and pray that after reading this book, you will get to understand what the Lord wants you to do in your life. All those experiences that we encountered, whether good or bad, are things that we can look back to, ponder upon, and learn from, for us to become better persons. Those unfortunate circumstances in our lives didn't happen for no reason. God, in his almighty power and ultimate wisdom, allows us to experience things in life that we can use to minister to others who are in need. Let me end this chapter with a wonderful poem that I came across while writing this book, which I think very well capture the essence of God's anointing to most of us. It is unfortunate that there is no identified authorship as I would have cited it properly. I tried searching as to who could have copyrighted this poem, but I cannot find any, so like most other writers, I would quote this poem under anonymous authorship.

> *When God wants to drill a man, and thrill a man,*
> * and skill a man,*
> *When God wants to mold a man, to play the noblest*
> * part;*
> *When He yearns with all His heart, to create so*
> * great and bold a man*
> *That all the world shall be amazed, watch His*
> * methods, watch His ways!*
> *How He ruthlessly perfects Whom He royally elects!*
> *How He hammers him and hurts him, and with*
> * mighty blows converts him.*
> *Into trial shapes of clay which Only God understands;*
> *While his tortured heart is crying, and he lifts*
> * beseeching hands!*
> *How He bends but never breaks, when his good He*
> * undertakes;*
> *How He uses whom He chooses, and which every*
> * purpose fuses him;*
> *By every act induces him To try His splendor out,*
> *God knows what He's about.*

I pray that the Lord's anointing be upon you and your cup overflows. Our psalmist, King David, who wrote the Twenty-Third Psalm, has well responded to God's anointing in his life. Acts 13:36 tells us, *"Now when David had served God's purpose in his own generation, he fell asleep; he was buried with his ancestors and his body decayed.*" I hope and pray that when we all leave this earth, the same can be said about us that we have fulfilled God's anointing in our lives.

Reflection Questions

1. Are you presently involved in any ministry? Are you serving in the church or somewhere else?
2. Have you been patiently waiting for God's call or are you currently doing what you think He wants you to do?
3. On a scale of 1 to 10, with 10 being the highest, how do you rate yourself concerning your response and commitment to God's calling in your life?

Dwelling in Your House

Surely goodness and lovingkindness will follow me
all the days of my life.
And I will dwell in the house of the Lord forever.

—Psalm 23:6

Finally, you are in the last chapter! Thank you for patiently going through the pages of this book. I hope and pray that your journey of reading and meditating on the Twenty-Third Psalm is all worth your time. This final chapter is your destination and mine, and that is to finally dwell in the house of the Lord!

There is one story in the life of King David that inspires me the most. From the earlier chapters of this book, we learned that King Saul who was King David's predecessor have spent quite a considerable length of time and a great deal of effort trying to chase King David wherever he went as he wanted to kill him. King David had been treated harshly by King Saul, and this all emanated from the latter's jealousy over the successful exploits of the former. First Samuel 18:6–9 tells us that on one occasion:

> *When David returned from killing the Philistine,*
> *the women came out of all the cities of Israel, sing-*
> *ing and dancing, to meet King Saul, playing songs*
> *of joy on timbrels. The women sang as they played,*
> *and said, "Saul has killed his thousands, and David*
> *his ten thousands." Then Saul became very angry.*
> *This saying did not please him. He said, "They have*
> *given David honor for ten thousands, but for me*

only thousands. Now what more can he have but
to be king?" And Saul was jealous and did not trust
David from that day on.

It was jealousy at its worst. It has corrupted the mind of King Saul and created envy in his heart. One time when King David was playing the harp for King Saul, the jealous king threw a spear at King David although he was able to jump out of it twice. Since then, King Saul had always been in pursuit of King David. He was hunting him like a wild animal, and this spirit of jealousy and envy have slowly consumed King Saul's rational thinking. He cannot function effectively as a king anymore. All he thought of was how to eliminate King David and get him out of his way.

Have you met people in your life who became so jealous of you to the point that they like to harm you, or they enjoy seeing you fail in every aspect of your life? God has given King Saul so much. He blessed him tremendously being king of Israel, but he strayed away from Him. He lets his jealousy ruin his relationship with his God and gave the enemy a foothold in his mind. The right attitude that God expects from us is that we should be happy when others succeed. We should not harbor ill feelings with those who are accomplishing well in life. I don't understand why some people feel bad when others succeed. A lot of times, God gives us the opportunity to handle a ministry in His church. If we don't give it our best shot, God can easily pass the opportunity to somebody else. God certainly does not need our talents and skills to accomplish the work that He wants to be done in His ministry. When God calls us to do something for Him, it is a privilege that we should be thankful for. This is precisely what happened between King Saul and King David. God gave King Saul several opportunities to prove himself worthy of being king of Israel, but he kept on failing God. He certainly blew up the multiple chances that were given to him. In the course of King Saul's pursuit of King David, the latter had several opportunities to kill King Saul. He might have thought of fighting back. Anyway, he was anointed to be the next king, but he did not take advantage of those opportunities, but instead, he chose not to touch the Lord's anointed and just waited for God's perfect timing when he could finally be king over all of Israel. There was one occasion when King David just cut off a piece of King Saul's clothing when the king was sleeping. He wanted to prove to King Saul that he came to him that close, and yet he did not lay a hand on him. There was one person who was a witness to King Saul's unfair treatment of King David. This was King Saul's own son Jonathan who incidentally was King David's closest friend. Jonathan had warned King David several times about his father King Saul and how he was really serious in trying to kill him. Jonathan was a true friend of King David.

In their battle with the Philistines on Mount Gilboa at the Jezreel Valley, both King Saul and Jonathan were killed. King David mourned the death of his friend Jonathan and even at the death of King Saul. At this time, all the members of King Saul's household panicked upon hearing the terrible news

We must remember that sometimes in this life, even well-meaning people can hurt us unintentionally.

and that the soldiers are coming to annihilate all of King Saul's families. The midwife who was taking care of the five-year-old Mephibosheth ran hysterically, picked up the young Mephibosheth in her effort to save him but unintentionally dropped him. This accident crippled Mephibosheth's feet for life. Every time the name of Mephibosheth is mentioned in the Bible, the phrase "who was crippled in both feet" followed. It has become his stigma all his life. It has become a permanent disability and a source of terrible shame for him. Mephibosheth lived in poverty since then and hid in an impoverished town called Lo-Debar (which literally means "no pasture.") Mephibosheth barely had anything to eat. One seemingly ordinary day, King David suddenly asked his servants if there is still any surviving family of King Saul that he can show his kindness to. This may sound arbitrary, but I believe God has caused King David to remember. One of the servants told him about Mephibosheth, son of Jonathan and grandson of King Saul. Upon learning that Mephibosheth was Jonathan's son, King David immediately sent his soldiers to Lo Debar and picked up Mephibosheth. I cannot imagine how fearful Mephibosheth could have been at the mere sight of King

David's soldiers. Isn't this king the reason for all his misery in life? He probably thought that King David finally found him, and he probably wanted him to pay for the sins of his grandfather King Saul. When Mephibosheth met King David, his initial statement, which can be found in 2 Samuel 9:8 was, *"What is your servant, that you should notice a dead dog like me?"* Mephibosheth had suffered all his life for something that he had nothing to do. The midwife did not mean him any harm. We must remember that sometimes in this life, even well-meaning people can hurt us unintentionally. Mephibosheth had nothing to do with the animosity between his grandfather King Saul and King David. Maybe Mephibosheth remembered how life was when his grandfather Saul was the king. Life would have been much better then. But this time, he was destitute, crippled from both feet and about to pay the price. He probably thinks it is better if he would just die. After all, he seemed dead already for a long time with all his sufferings.

How many of us have been suffering the consequences of things that we did not have any direct or even indirect participation in? Sins of our ancestors still creeps toward several generations and those innocent descendants suffer. How many of us have been hurt by well-meaning people? They have good intentions, but nevertheless, they hurt us. This was not the end of story for Mephibosheth. King David told him that he summoned him not to punish him but to bless him. King David has not forgotten about him. He gave him all the properties that once belonged to his grandfather King Saul and he asked servants to work for Mephibosheth. The most surprising of all, King David invited Mephibosheth to eat with him in the king's table. This is probably the highest honor any one can attain during those times. King David told Mephibosheth that from that time on, he will eat at the king's table. King David restored Mephibosheth's status being part of the royal family.

In our lives, we may have been crippled by so many things—by our sins, by our inabilities, by our shortcomings, and sometimes, we suffer consequences of sins we didn't even commit. We may have been hiding in our own Lo Debars—no pasture, impoverished, afraid, miserable, and probably a lot of times we are on the verge of giving up. The important thing to remember is that the Good Shepherd never forgets us, and sometimes God blesses us because of His promise to our fathers or grandfathers or great-grandfathers. He remembers us for who we truly are, and He plans to call us back and bring us into the flock. Just like King David remembering his friendship with Jonathan, God remembers us through the righteousness of Jesus Christ. Only God can restore our position in His kingdom. Just like Mephibosheth, God wants to restore us and for us to dine with Him and have fellowship with Him for eternity in His royal table. The Good Shepherd wants us to dwell in His house forever!

There is no greater blessing of being in a relationship with the Shepherd than the Shepherd Himself. Our ultimate reward is God and our fellowship with Him for the rest of our days. We need to feel His daily presence in our lives and "taste" His goodness. What King David is trying to tell us in this last verse of the Twenty-Third Psalm is the reality of the blessing that awaits a person who has truly surrendered his life to the Good Shepherd. His reward is the Shepherd Himself—His goodness, His lovingkindness, His mercy, His grace, and His blessings. King David used the word *surely*, and it only means being so assured and being so certain about it. He doesn't have any doubt that the Good Shepherd can do those things for him. He is saying that God's lovingkindness and goodness pursue him all his life. His goodness follows us everywhere we go in this life or even in the life to come. It is like a persistent traffic police officer who tried to pursue someone who violated a traffic rule. But, of course, God's lovingkindness and goodness do not pursue us like that. The Bible tells us in 1 John 4:7–9, "*Dear friends, let us love one another, for love comes from God. Everyone who loves has been born of God and knows God. Whoever does not love does not know God, because God is love. This is how God showed his love among us: He sent his one and only Son into the world that we might live through him.*" God is love. He is not just practicing love or symbolizing love or teaching us how to love. God is love. He is the complete embodiment of the term. Being in love with God is a blessing that guarantees a person

> There is no greater blessing of being in a relationship with the Shepherd than the Shepherd Himself.

who is a sheep to the Good Shepherd. Other versions of the Bible use the term *mercy* instead of *love* or *loving kindness*. Mercy is one of God's attributes, which simply means that He does not let us get what we deserve. It's the perfect illustration of God's love in action. Whenever Jesus looks at His sheep, He has compassion on us. He knows that we are helpless, and on our own, we are not capable of doing anything without His help. When He saw the multitude of people following Him, He had compassion on them because they are helpless like a flock of sheep without a shepherd. He wasn't just sorry for all people. God's mercy is more than just feeling sorry, but it is a kind of emotion that is coupled with action, and that action is doing something to really help someone out.

Our life here on earth is limited, and it has to be well spent. Some people say our life here on earth is simply a test as to where we shall spend our next life. If we pass the test, we shall be with God for eternity. If we fail the test, we shall be separated from God for eternity. Although the Gospel is available for everyone, Jesus Himself said that there will be fewer people who will pass the test. This is the sad and fearful reality. Jesus said in

> The advancement of technology, science and medicine seem to pull people away from the fundamental belief that there is a Divine Authority, the Creator of everything who has been there even before time began.

Matthew 7:13, "*Enter through the narrow gate. For wide is the gate and broad is the road that leads to destruction, and many enter through it.*" It's very hard to visualize that there will be more people who will reject Christ and are bound for destruction. This reality tells us that the rule of the majority is not always right. Majority of people of all ages, all throughout history, will be rejecting God, and less people will be saved. We can tell from what's going on in our world today that more and more people are not only rejecting Christ but denying the fact that there is God. We have heard in the news that even in America, prayers are no longer allowed in many public schools. Our children in schools are bombarded with ideas that there is no God and our existence here on earth is a mere product of random chance through evolution or other unfounded theories. The advancement of technology, science and medicine seem to pull people away from the fundamental belief that there is a Divine Authority, the Creator of everything who has been there even before time began. Even if the Gospel is not specifically shared to someone, I believe that each person will be given the opportunity to meet God in a personal way. The Bible tells us in Romans 1:20, *"For since the creation of the world God's invisible qualities—his eternal power and divine nature—have been clearly seen, being understood from what has been made, so that people are without excuse."* All we need to do is look around us and marvel at God's creation or look within our own selves and see how He has structured the human body from our five senses deep down into the structure of our DNA. These are enough and obvious reasons to convince anyone that there is God. If we have surrendered our lives to the Good Shepherd, King David said that His lovingkindness and goodness will follow us all the days of our lives. This is very important because there are times we question God why it seems that we are alone in our life's journey. There are times in our lives that we feel God has left us or God has abandoned us. It reminds me of this wonderful poem "Footprints in the Sand" where the writer asked God why is it that during his lowest and darkest hours, he seemed to only see one set of footprints in the sand and he thought God has left him. And we know how God responded that during those times he saw one set of footprints, God was indeed carrying him. I believe that, not literally but figuratively. God indeed carry us through our darkest days. He takes our burden and lifts us up. He is always there. He promised not to leave nor forsake us. The Bible says in Deuteronomy 31:8, *"Be strong and courageous. Do not be afraid or terrified because of them, for the* LORD *your God goes with you; he will never leave you nor forsake you."* The Good Shepherd promises to be with us all the days of our lives.

Another blessing of being a sheep of the Good Shepherd is our fellowship with Him. The Bible says in Revelation 3:20, *"Here I am! I stand at the door and knock. If anyone hears my voice and opens the door, I will come in and eat with that person, and they with me."* This verse speaks of a fellowship with the Good Shepherd. Dining with someone is one of the most intimate experience we can have. The last verse of the Twenty-Third Psalm gives the final conclusion that whether we see God as our Good Shepherd or we see God as a gracious and loving host, what is important is the main theme of this psalm that is plain and simple: King David is telling us and he is describing what a joy we can surely have if we have a personal and intimate relationship with the Lord, a kind of relationship that will outlive anyone or anything here on earth. Our relationship with the Good Shepherd is like no other, and it has no end. The Twenty-Third Psalm portrays our lives here on earth as a journey, a pilgrimage. It is a pilgrimage where the Good Shepherd stays with us every step of the way. It is a pilgrimage with God toward God. Our final destination is to dwell in *the house of the Lord forever.* Our final destination is an unhindered and intimate fellowship with Jesus Christ in heaven. This is the ultimate hope of every person who placed his or her trust on the Good Shepherd here on earth. And this hope toward getting to our final destination should define everything that we do here on earth in the meantime. Whether we are talking about secular work or ministry work such as Bible studies, building project, or children's programs, these things are not the main reason why we were doing them. And any church program or project that does not bring us toward a much better relationship with the Good Shepherd is a misguided project and misses the point of why we are doing all those things in the first place. It is time for us to examine the purposes that are behind the things that we undertake and go back to the main reason why we're doing it in the first place. The Apostle Paul tells us in 1 Corinthians 13:13, *"And now these three remain: faith, hope and love. But the greatest of these is love."* While here on earth, we walk by faith, and we need faith to move on against all the challenges and problems of this life. Faith, as defined in Hebrews 11:1 is, *"Now faith is confidence in what we hope for and assurance about what we do not see."* When we get to heaven, we see our Lord face-to-face, and we shall be with him for eternity so faith is no longer necessary. Hope also keeps us going. Our hope that one day Jesus Christ will come back and take us with Him helps us persevere against our trials and keep us motivated to live our lives to the full. When we get to heaven, the hope that we had while we were on earth will turn into reality, so hope ends there. But love, it goes on forever. With God, love will always be there because He is love, whether here on earth and someday in heaven. When we reach our final destination, when we get to the house of the Lord, there will be no more religiosity nor traditions, but what will remain is our loving relationship with the Good Shepherd.

This last verse reminds me of the flock of sheep who have been going to different pastures. The flock of sheep goes through all those places—in the valleys, in dark ravines, in green pastures, by the lakeside. In all of these destinations, the flock is with the shepherd. He never leaves them as he leads them wherever he goes. He is with them in their abundance when they find green pastures and quiet waters, and he is with them during their lack when they walk through the valleys, deep ravines, and mountains. At one point, they will all go back to the Shepherd's real home where they have their permanent dwelling. This is the flock's final destination. Similarly, in our life's pilgrimage, we go through ups and downs. Figuratively speaking, we climb up on the mountains; we pass through dark ravines; we encounter ferocious wolves and lions along the way; we walk through the valleys; and we reach green pastures and drink on quiet waters. The mountains, ravines, wolves, and lions can represent the challenges that we face—daunting problems, crisis, disasters, lingering sicknesses, frustrations, and disappointments. Walking through the valleys can represent standstills and plateaus in our lives. Nothing much happening, and we barely hear anything from God, or so we thought. In other times, the green pastures and quiet waters are times of success and victory: problems are solved, sicknesses are healed, material prosperity is achieved, and other accomplishments. This is how our lives fan out very much. The important thing to recognize and acknowledge is that the Good Shepherd is always with us no matter what. Our ultimate hope is that no matter how long and arduous the journey is, we shall one day reach our final destination. We shall dwell in the house of our Lord forever.

> **How you view the end-times, life after death, and eternity depends on your understanding of the Scripture.**

The Bible talks a lot about the end of days. Sometimes, we get to wonder how this world that we know is going to end especially when we hear news about possibilities of nuclear war, terrorism, global warming, earthquakes, and tsunamis. Whenever we confront these kinds of newsflash day after day, we end up longing and wishing that the end will truly come. How you view the end-times, life after death, and eternity depends on your understanding of the Scripture. I believe what the Bible says that Jesus Christ promised to come back for His flock, and He does this with no announcement like a thief in the night and in the twinkling of an eye. This is called the *rapture,* which literally means "snatched away or being caught up in the air." Only those who have received the Good Shepherd in their lives as Lord and Savior will be part of this event. Christ will not descend to earth at this time but will only come in the clouds to "snatch away" all those people who trust and believe in Him. Those who are dead in Christ will be resurrected first, and those who are still alive will immediately be transformed, and both shall have glorified bodies designed to last for eternity. Jesus will then take His saints back to heaven. First Thessalonians 4:16–17 tells us that *"the Lord himself will come down from heaven, with a loud command, with the voice of the archangel and with the trumpet call of God, and the dead in Christ will rise first. After that, we who are still alive and are left will be caught up together with them in the clouds to meet the Lord in the air. And so we will be with the Lord forever."* Jesus Christ will be like a bridegroom who came back from His Father's house to pick up His bride. Jesus said in John 14:2–3, *"My Father's house has many rooms; if that were not so, would I have told you that I am going there to prepare a place for you? And if I go and prepare a place for you, I will come back and take you to be with me that you also may be where I am."* Jesus was actually using the metaphor of a bridegroom wherein according to old Jewish traditions about marriage, usually a year earlier, the bride gets engaged to the bridegroom, but the bridegroom had to leave for a while and go back to his father's house to prepare the place that they will eventually live as a couple. I believe that Jesus Christ seating at the right hand of the Father is not only interceding for us in prayer, but He is also preparing that place right now. During the *rapture* when Jesus takes His saints to heaven, there will be terrible things happening here on earth. The Bible also tells us that the *rapture* shall trigger the seven-year tribulation here on earth where the Antichrist will rise and deceive many people. He will gain control of the whole world and will greatly persecute many people. There will be great famines and wars that will cause great devastation and depression here on earth. Crime rates will escalate, and more and more people will be denied of justice and worst, killed. Come to think of it, Christians are called in the Bible as the "salt of the Earth." Matthew 5:13 tells us (Jesus speaking), *"You are the salt of the earth. But if the salt loses its saltiness, how can it be made salty again?"* We know that this world and its ways are referred to as "flesh," and *salt* has been traditionally used especially in the old days as a preservative especially for meat. Without salt, the meat decays. Anything the world has to offer appeals only to our flesh. Only God can totally change our spirit; hence, Christ's true followers are called born again of the Spirit. If the Christians are taken away during the *rapture*, the salt of the earth is taken away, then obviously this world, like flesh, will start to rot. I believe the reason why this world functions as it is right now is mainly because of Christians. Any follower of Christ is expected to show love and mercy, justice and fairness among all people. Without the Christians (i.e. during the tribulation period), the world will deteriorate at her lowest level.

At the end of the seven-year tribulation, Jesus Christ will finally return as a great and conquering King along with His mighty angels and the previously "raptured" saints. Known as the battle of Armageddon, He will defeat the Antichrist and his followers, and He will bound Satan into the bottomless pit for the next one thousand years. This is called the Second Coming or the Second Advent of Christ. This significant event ushers in the millennial kingdom where Jesus Himself will rule the world, and Jerusalem will be the capital and the center of worship. This is a period of perfect government as Christ is physically ruling the world, along with His angels and saints. The

> **Sin creeps from within the heart of every man, and the only solution to sin is spiritual rebirth in Christ.**

world will achieve peace and unmatched prosperity during this time. There will be no deception coming from the archenemy of God as Satan is bound in the abyss for one thousand years. At the end of the millennial kingdom, Satan will be released from the bottomless pit for a short time, and he will still deceive many. This tells us that sin can still abound even under a perfect environment where Christ rules and Satan is bound. Sin creeps from within the heart of every man, and the only solution to sin is spiritual rebirth in Christ. Those people who constantly reject Christ during His millennial reign will join Satan in a final rebellion, but our Lord shall quickly end it, and Satan will be cast into the lake of fire, never to bother anyone again, for eternity. God will then make a complete makeover of this world including the heavens. It is called the New Heavens and the New Earth. On the New Earth is a great city called the New Jerusalem. This is the final destination of God's flock. This is the place of ultimate comfort, joy, and glory as we will live with the Lord for eternity. The New Jerusalem is the green pasture that never runs out of abundance and the quiet waters that never runs dry. It is at this time that God will wipe away all tears, no more mourning or weeping, no more pain or death, no more sorrow. This is our eternal state, our final destination. King David, and so shall all of us, have that ultimate hope that this is what we meant by "dwelling in the house of the Lord forever." It does not talk about here and now. It talks about the afterward. It talks about eternity.

Don't miss the point of the Twenty-Third Psalm. Our Good Shepherd, Jesus Christ, calls each one us, not to be occupied by empty rituals and shallow activities but to be involved in having a true and authentic relationship with Him. If we get into this kind of relationship with the Good Shepherd, He gets the glory He truly deserves, and we get the true joy that we so desperately try to find. It's so amazing that King David, who used to be a shepherd, has compared himself to be a sheep in the Twenty-Third Psalm. He has complete dependency on the Good Shepherd. The Lord Jesus, whom King David called as his Shepherd and in the New Testament, Jesus called Himself the Good Shepherd now becomes the lamb. He's no ordinary lamb, He is the Lamb of God who takes away the sins of the world. At the cross in Calvary, Jesus has paid for your sins and mine.

Jesus has elaborated the Shepherd and sheep metaphor in different verses of chapter 10 of the Gospel of John. In this tenth chapter of John, Jesus used not only one but two metaphors about Himself. He calls Himself the gate where sheep would enter, and He calls Himself the Good Shepherd who is ready to lay down His life for His sheep. He said from verses 2 to 17:

> *The one who enters by the gate is the shepherd of the sheep. The gatekeeper opens the gate for him, and the sheep listen to his voice. He calls his own sheep by name and leads them out. When he has brought out all his own, he goes on ahead of them, and his sheep follow him because they know his voice. But they will never follow a stranger; in fact, they will run away from him because they do not recognize a stranger's voice.*

Therefore, Jesus said again, "Very truly I tell you, I am the gate for the sheep.

> *All who have come before me are thieves and robbers, but the sheep have not listened to them. I am the gate; whoever enters through me will be saved. They will come in and go out, and find pasture. The thief comes only to steal and kill and destroy; I have come that they may have life, and have it to the full.*
>
> *"I am the good shepherd. The good shepherd lays down his life for the sheep. The hired hand is not the shepherd and does not own the sheep. So when he sees the wolf coming, he abandons the sheep and runs away. Then the wolf attacks the flock and scatters it."*
>
> *The man runs away because he is a hired hand and cares nothing for the sheep. "I am the*

good shepherd; I know my sheep and my sheep know me— just as the Father knows me and I know the Father—and I lay down my life for the sheep.

"I have other sheep that are not of this sheep pen. I must bring them also. They too will listen to my voice, and there shall be one flock and one shepherd. The reason my Father loves me is that I lay down my life—only to take it up again. No one takes it from me, but I lay it down of my own accord. I have authority to lay it down and authority to take it up again. This command I received from my Father."

As you come to the close of reading through this final chapter, I would like to share some of the most important Christian doctrines that is very useful for those who will eventually decide to follow Jesus and for those who are already with Him but needs to strengthen what they believe. It is also very useful as we share the Gospel of Christ to others. "Dwelling in Your House" does not only mean to be literally dwelling in the Lord's abode, but it also means being part of His household or His flock while we are still here on Earth.

The ultimate source of truth and authority is God's Word, the Bible, which is the inspired and infallible word of God. We must believe in faith that this book is God-breathed and the writers, while they were allowed by God to manifest their writing styles, were divinely inspired by no less than the Holy Spirit Himself. It is through this inspiration that the Holy Spirit guided them on what to write.

There is only one God, the Creator of everything, the Good Shepherd. He has revealed Himself in three coeternal, distinct persons—God the Father, God the Son (who is Jesus Christ), and the Holy Spirit. Our God is omniscient, omnipotent, and omnipresent. He is holy and full of mercy, grace, and love.

Jesus Christ is God's visible representation here on earth. He is God incarnate, 100 percent man and 100 percent God. He provided the way to salvation of man by dying on the cross on our behalf.

He was conceived of the Holy Spirit through the Virgin Mary. Jesus lived a perfect and sinless life, which makes Him the only qualified sacrifice to redeem us. He was crucified, died, buried, and on the third day, He rose again proving to everyone that He has conquered death. He ascended to heaven and is now seated at the right hand of God the Father.

The Holy Spirit, unlike what other people think, is not just a force but a person. He indwells believers and convicts us when we commit sins and enlightens our hearts especially when we study God's Word. He is the seal promised by the Father to every believer. He is our Comforter, our Counsellor.

Mankind is created by God and was made in His image and likeness. When God created everything else, He said it is good, but when He created man, He said it was very good. Because of Adam's fall, humanity has inherited a sinful nature, which offends God and breaks our relationship with Him. We are saved and this relationship is restored because of God's grace through faith in Christ through His victory on the cross. Salvation is received by any man by grace alone, through faith alone, and in Christ alone. Grace is the locus of our faith. A true child of God does not perform good works to be saved, but good works is a natural fruit or evidence that we are saved already.

The church or the body of Christ or the Lord's flock is made up of Christ's followers, and it is very important and a command that we participate in the activities of the church. Through the church, we learn how to love each other, pray for each other, support each other, rejoice with each other, and correct each other. Our mission is to fulfill the Great Commission of Jesus Christ, which is to share the Gospel and make disciples of all nations.

One day Jesus will come back for His saints in an event called the *rapture* where His followers will be taken by Him to heaven. After seven years, Jesus will come again with His saints and angel to fight in the battle of Armageddon and eventually establish the millennial kingdom. All humanity will have the physical resurrection. Those who received Jesus will experience dwelling in His house for eternity, while those who rejected Him will be sent to the eternal lake of fire and be punished forever.

My own mother had struggled with colon cancer for the past seven years. Her last two years were tough as she battled the effects of radiation treatment when she was eighty years old. The radiation treatment had damaged her brain, which severely affected her ability to talk and eat through her mouth. The year she passed away, God has blessed me with the privilege of visiting her in the Philippines a month before she died. My office sent me for work, and I took a side trip to our hometown for a few days. Even for a few days, I was able to be with her, reading her a Filipino Bible and singing songs for her. My mom had responded to invitations to receive Christ a couple of times, and she had prayed the sinner's prayer during those occasions. I believe in my heart that she has accepted Jesus in her life. She wasn't able to talk to me, but I know she understood each word that I said and read to her. I am so grateful with my family who selflessly took care of her until her last moment. My oldest sister had sacrificed a lot to take care of my mother, same with my other sister, my late brother, my sister-in-law, and my nephews. They took turns in looking after my own mother especially during those times she needed it the most. I can say I am still so blessed that my mother was looked after by people whom she loved. In other places, seniors are taken cared of by other people, not necessarily by their loved ones. In the case of my mom, she was looked after mainly by my sister, who is a nurse, and this is probably one of the greatest blessings that I would always thank the Lord for. I remember reading the Twenty-Third psalm to my mother in *Filipino* language.

My mom passed away a month after I last visited her. I can still feel her hands on my hands, her smell, and her stare as if she wanted to say something, but her brain was no longer capable to forming the words. I believe the moment she died, she immediately dwelt in the house of our Lord. Her pain is gone; her health is restored; and her speech ability came back. I thank God for her and for the wonderful memories that she has given our whole family.

If your parents are still alive as you are reading this book, call them and tell them you love them. Do not wait until the time they can no longer speak or lying on their deathbeds or when you are thousands of miles apart. For the longest time, we have dwelt in the house of our parents, and they have sacrificed a lot for each one of us. I hope and pray that this book will remind everyone how God manifested His love for each one of us through our parents.

After all that has been written and explained in this book, we can go back to that kindergarten boy who was asked to recite the Twenty-Third Psalm. He said, *"The Lord is my shepherd, that's all I need to know."* True enough, after learning all these things, the most important thing is for Jesus Christ to become your Good Shepherd. And that's all you need to know! I hope and pray that you have learned enough from this book and as you are convicted by the Holy Spirit to make a decision to receive Jesus. The next chapter is an invitation for you. If all your life you have been searching and has never surrendered your life to the lordship of Jesus Christ, I urge you to read the next chapter of this book, and I pray that you will respond to God's call with willingness and with a genuine heart to follow Him.

David looks beyond the green pasture in the days to come. He was inspired by the panorama of dwelling in the house of the Lord forever. The Hebrew expression "forever" defines a present reality that continues into the future. As each one of us walk along the path of the Good Shepherd here on earth, we shall eventually dwell in His house.

If you have responded positively to the Good Shepherd's call and you accepted Him the Lord and Savior of your life, surely, His goodness and love will follow you all the days of your life. Solely by His grace, you can be sure that you will dwell in His house forever.

Reflection Questions

1. What is your idea of dwelling in the house of the Lord?
2. Do you think you will enjoy being in His company in heaven for eternity?
3. Are you in a difficult situation now that you feel the Good Shepherd has forgotten about you?

An Invitation

This book is all about understanding our relationship with the Good Shepherd. Are you already part of His flock? Have you made Jesus your Good Shepherd? Do you recognize His voice? Do you follow His leading? Do you "smell" like Him, and are you familiar with His ways?

If you are not sure how to answer these questions, it's all right. There is one thing I can assure you, though: God loves you and that is a fact, and He certainly wants you to experience true peace and abundance. The Bible tells us that *"we have peace with God through Jesus Christ"* (Rom. 5:1). The reason why you have not fully experienced true peace and abundance in your life is because of sin.

Sin separates us from God. How can all-loving God create somebody who sins? Well, God created each one of us so we can love Him back. This love is something He won't force upon anybody. He gave us free will. There is nothing wrong with you if you have sinned. Everyone sins! The Bible tells us in Romans 3:23, *"For all have sinned and fall short of the glory of God."* As we exercise our free will, we make choices each day either to follow God or to disobey Him. Because of sin, there is a gulf between us and God. While most people try to reach God through good works or even through religious activities or through philosophy or even science, these are all futile attempts. There is no way we can bridge that gulf and reach God. Because of God's great love for us, He Himself devised a plan to bridge that gulf. That plan involves His only begotten Son, Jesus Christ.

Jesus Christ is God's only provision to bridge that gulf. The Bible tells us in 1 Timothy 2:5, *"For there is one God and one Mediator between God and men, the Man Jesus Christ."* Jesus Himself said in

John 3:16, *"For God so loved the world that he gave his one and only Son, that whoever believes in him shall not perish but have eternal life,"* and in John 14:6, He continued by saying, *"I am the Way, the Truth and the Life. No one comes to the Father except through Me."* Now the choice is yours. Will you follow Jesus and cross that bridge toward God or remain in your sinful state of eternal separation from God?

Will you receive Jesus as your personal Savior and follow Him as Lord? The Bible tells us that *"if you confess with your mouth that Jesus is Lord and believe in your heart that God raised Him from the dead, you will be saved!"* (Rom. 10:9).

You can receive Jesus through a prayer today. You can be part of the flock that is being taken care of by the Good Shepherd. You can be part of His family. You can be a child of the Most High God. I hope that God will use this book to touch your life and be prompted by the Holy Spirit to make that important decision.

I sincerely believe that if you pray the following prayer genuinely from your heart and make it as your own prayer, you will be saved. The prayer goes like this:

> *Heavenly Father, I admit that I am a sinner, and I ask for Your forgiveness today. Today I open my heart and life to Your Only Begotten Son, Jesus Christ. I believe that He was crucified, and He died on the cross so He could pay for my sins. I believe that He conquered death by rising up again after three days. Today, I accept Him as my Savior and Lord. I pray that the Holy Spirit will minister in my life from this day on and make me the kind of person that You want me to be.*
>
> *In Jesus's name. Amen.*

If you have prayed that prayer from your heart, I praise God for your decision to receive Jesus in your life. You may also want to write on the space below your name and the date you have accepted the Good Shepherd in your life as it is a very important event. It is the best and the most important decision that you have ever made in your life.

Your Name: _____ Date: _____

I also hope and pray that you will share this good news of salvation to your friends and loved ones.

If you may, please write me an e-mail at ramilcarmen@gmail.com, if this book has touched your life, one way or the other. God bless you!

In Christ,

Pastor Ramil Carmen

British Columbia, Canada

Scripture Verses Quoted

Preface

- Romans 11:36
- Hebrews 4:12

Introduction

- John 10:27
- Romans 8:28
- Genesis 50:20

A Man After God's Own Heart

- Genesis 20:2
- Exodus 4:10–12
- 1 Samuel 16:12
- 1 Samuel 16:7
- 1 Samuel 19:2
- 1 Samuel 17:26
- Hebrews 11:6
- James 1:2–4
- 2 Samuel 11:1
- Psalms 139:1–4
- Matthew 7:5

The Twenty-Third Psalm

- Psalm 23:1–6

The Good Shepherd and His Sheep

- John 4:24
- Matthew 23:12
- Isaiah 40:11
- Psalm 80:1
- Hebrews 13:20
- Genesis 1:27
- Philippians 2:5–11
- 1 Corinthians 3:19
- Psalm 14:1
- John 15:15
- Ecclesiastes 4:9–10
- Psalm 133:1
- Ephesians 1:7
- Proverbs 3:5–6
- Genesis 22:13
- John 1:29
- Isaiah 40:8
- James 3:1
- John 13:35

Jehovah Jireh: God Is Our Provider

- John 15:5
- Philippians 4:19
- Matthew 6:9–13
- Matthew 6:33
- 2 Chronicles 1:7–12
- 1 Corinthians 1:18
- Genesis 22:14
- Matthew 5:45

- Matthew 19:16–22
- 2 Corinthians 12:9
- 1 Corinthians 13:11
- Matthew 6:34
- Galatians 6:4–5
- 1 Timothy 6:6–11

Peace and Abundance in the Lord

- John 6:35
- Luke 2:17
- Psalm 139:1–3
- Matthew 11:28–30
- John 14:27
- Philippians 4:6–7
- Psalm 121:4
- Psalm 24:1
- John 10:10
- 1 Corinthians 2:9

What Profit Is a Man?

- Genesis 2:7
- John 12:27
- Luke 22:43
- Luke 10:42
- 1 Peter 4:9–11
- Ecclesiastes 2:22–23
- Isaiah 43:7
- Colossians 3:23
- Proverbs 22:6
- Matthew 16:26
- Matthew 10:28
- Isaiah 64:6
- Mark 9:35
- Mark 9:37

- Proverbs 14:12
- 2 Timothy 4:7

Death Is but a Shadow

- John 15:4–6
- Ecclesiastes 4:12
- Malachi 2:16
- 1 Peter 5:8
- Luke 19:10
- 2 Corinthians 4:17
- Hosea 4:6
- Corinthians 15:55–57
- Hebrews 9:27
- Revelation 21:4
- 1 John 4:4
- 1 Timothy 6:7
- Ecclesiastes 7:2

Rod or Staff: Which One Do You Choose?

- Numbers 17:8
- Numbers 20:8
- Numbers 20:12
- Romans 13:1
- 1 Samuel 8:6–11
- Proverbs 21:1
- Proverbs 29:15
- 2 Samuel 7:14
- Proverbs 13:24
- Isaiah 53:6
- 1 John 2:16
- Romans 5:8
- 1 Peter 5:2–4

Behind Enemy Lines

- Romans 12:12
- John 16:33
- 1 John 1:9
- John 10:28
- Hebrews 6:4–6
- Psalm 51:12a
- Luke 23:34
- Proverbs 17:17
- 1 John 4:4
- Ephesians 6:12
- Matthew 5:44
- Luke 6:29
- Ephesians 6:17
- Matthew 4:3
- Deuteronomy 8:3

God's Anointing and Our Overflowing Cup

- Mark 6:13
- James 5:14
- Mark 14:3–9
- Hebrews 1:8–9
- Galatians 6:10
- Ephesians 5:18
- Galatians 5:22–23
- Proverbs 16:18
- James 4:6
- Galatians 4:4
- John 1:11
- 2 Peter 3:9
- Matthew 24:14
- Psalm 130:5–6

Dwelling in Your House

- 1 Samuel 18:6–9
- 2 Samuel 9:8
- 1 John 4:7–9
- Matthew 7:13
- Romans 1:20
- Deuteronomy 31:8
- Revelation 3:20
- 1 Corinthians 13:13
- Hebrews 11:1
- 1 Thessalonians 4:16–17
- John 14:2–3
- Matthew 5:13
- John 2:10–17

An Invitation

- Romans 5:1
- Romans 3:23
- 1 Timothy 2:5
- John 14:6
- Romans 10:9

Notes

[1] Harvey, Schmidt, "Try to Remember." Released 1965.
[2] C. S. Lewis, The Problem of Pain (The Centenary Press, 1940).
[3] The Bible Study Tools, 2008, https://www.biblestudytools.com/lexicons/greek.
[4] Rick Warren, Purpose Driven Life (Zondervan, 2002).

About the Author

Ramil N. Carmen is a pastor of Word Christian Community Church in New Westminster, British Columbia, Canada. He has been writing and preaching church sermons for more than ten years.

He has a bachelor's degree in business administration, a CPA and holds a master's degree in theology.

He is married to Eleanor Carmen and they were blessed with two children: Elaine and Ram. They live in Surrey, British Columbia, Canada.

He plays the guitar and loves to play scrabble with his family. His life verse is Matthew 16:26.

CPSIA information can be obtained
at www.ICGtesting.com
Printed in the USA
FSHW010819071119
63761FS